USN SUBMARINE
VS
IJN AIRCRAFT CARRIER

The Pacific 1942–44

MARK LARDAS

OSPREY PUBLISHING
Bloomsbury Publishing Plc
Kemp House, Chawley Park, Cumnor Hill, Oxford OX2 9PH, UK
29 Earlsfort Terrace, Dublin 2, Ireland
1385 Broadway, 5th Floor, New York, NY 10018, USA
E-mail: info@ospreypublishing.com
www.ospreypublishing.com

OSPREY is a trademark of Osprey Publishing Ltd

First published in Great Britain in 2025

A catalog record for this book is available from the British Library.

ISBN: PB 9781472862204; eBook 9781472862136;
ePDF 9781472862150; XML 9781472862143

25 26 27 28 29 10 9 8 7 6 5 4 3 2 1

Maps by bounford.com
Index by Rob Munro
Typeset by PDQ Digital Media Solutions, Bungay, UK
Printed by Repro India Ltd.

Osprey Publishing supports the Woodland Trust, the UK's leading woodland
conservation charity.

To find out more about our authors and books visit **www.ospreypublishing.com**.
Here you will find extracts, author interviews, details of forthcoming events and
the option to sign up for our newsletter.

Dedication
To Zeke Zelmer and the men of the Cavalla Association who allowed me to
attend their 2014 reunion.

Acknowledgments
I would like to thank Kelly Crooks, lead author of the book *Warships at
Seawolf Park*, and Seawolf Park in Galveston, Texas, for providing images of
Cavalla in World War II.

Author's note
The following abbreviations indicate the sources of the illustrations used in
this volume:

AC – Author's collection
AP-HMM – Author photograph taken at the Houston Maritime Museum
LOC – Library of Congress, Washington, DC
USNA – United States Naval Academy
USNHHC – United States Naval Heritage and History Command

Title-page photograph: Living conditions aboard a submarine were cramped.
Submariners ate and slept in the same compartment in close quarters. Crew
members had to get along with each other. (AC)

CONTENTS

INTRODUCTION

"The Japanese fleet was passing by the *Flying Fish* and appeared to be coming through the [San Bernardino] Strait," Elmer "Zeke" Zelmer, the communications officer aboard *Cavalla*, which was on its first war patrol, related in an interview he gave in 2014, 70 years after the boat sank the Japanese aircraft carrier *Shōkaku*:

At that point we were given another assignment; to cover that area and watch for the fleet. Eventually, after we found the fleet we let it pass by because we were instructed to report its location to our search forces. We were then assigned to another area and were again fortunate. Part of the fleet came into that area. That was when the First Battle of the Philippine Sea began. We were lucky during that period to get a Japanese carrier group come steaming through directly towards us and we were able to get close enough to shoot a full load of torpedoes and get three or four hits on the *Shōkaku*.

My battle station was conning officer. I took the information from the radar or the skipper's periscope sightings and plotted them versus our position. I then attempted to find over a period of several observations the target's compass [heading] and speed so we could maneuver into a position ahead of it and get in position close enough to shoot when she came by. So I was following the target's information.

The attack was about 11:00; the *Shōkaku* sank about 2½ hours later. About three in the afternoon, something like that, [we surfaced]. It was still daylight. As soon as we surfaced and it was clear, we started chasing after the direction the convoy went. We never did catch up with them. We were quite confident we sunk her because at a point about 2½ hours later we heard some distant explosions and a rumbling that carried on for some seconds. Depth charges went click-BANG, and were over. We thought that explosion was in fact the *Shōkaku*. We were pretty confident the attack sunk her.

A view of the IJN aircraft carrier *Taihō*. Sinking major enemy warships, especially aircraft carriers, was the dream of every submarine captain, one only ten USN captains achieved during the Pacific War. (AC)

Then when things had quieted down and we were on the surface we took out the medicinal whiskey and we made a cocktail of it if you will and everybody got a short glass of it. At that time it was a generic fleet carrier. We didn't know. We just knew we had a big Japanese carrier and she had planes on the forward deck when we fired on her.

Zelmer, Lieutenant Commander Herman J. Kossler (*Cavalla*'s skipper), and the rest of the men aboard *Cavalla* were unaware of the identity of their target at the time they sank it. It was not until they refueled at Saipan they learned it was the carrier *Shōkaku*. That made victory all the sweeter, because *Shōkaku* was one of six Japanese carriers that participated in the attack on Pearl Harbor on December 7, 1941. *Shōkaku* would be the only one of the six sunk by a US Navy (USN) submarine during the ensuing war.

Battles between submarines and aircraft carriers were very much David and Goliath contests. Submarines were among the smallest oceangoing naval combatants; so small that men of the Submarine Service called their vessels "boats," a tradition followed to this day. In contrast, carriers were among the largest oceangoing naval combatants; and they were faster than even a surfaced submarine.

An IJN aircraft carrier's view of an attacking USN fleet submarine, its periscope raised above the waterline. This is the night periscope, which featured a head larger and more visible than that of the daytime periscope. (USNHHC)

To attack a carrier successfully the submarine relied upon stealth, placing itself in a favorable position from which to launch its torpedoes. Then the interception solution for the torpedoes had to be accurate. US torpedoes moved at around the top speed of a carrier, which meant that if they were detected early enough the carrier could outrun them. Finally, the torpedoes had to explode when they struck the carrier.

Early in the war US torpedoes ran deeper than set, underrunning their target. Often when they did strike home the torpedo exploder failed when it hit, resulting in a dud. US torpedo warheads were smaller than those of other navies. The USN Bureau of Ordnance believed at least four hits were required to take down a ship the size of a carrier. Although skill was necessary to successfully sink a carrier, so was luck.

Only ten aircraft carriers of the Imperial Japanese Navy (IJN) were sunk by USN fleet submarines during World War II, each by a different submarine. All the sinkings took place between December 1943 and December 1944. Before that period the performance of US torpedoes was too unreliable. After December 1944, Japanese carriers largely remained in port or in waters USN submarines could not reach.

These battles captured the public imagination. The climax of every war movie that featured a USN submarine in World War II seemed to involve the sinking of a carrier, the submarine having been sent to a rendezvous point by radio message from Commander, Submarine Force, US Pacific Fleet (COMSUBPAC: Rear Admiral Robert H. English from May 14, 1942 through January 21, 1943; Vice Admiral Charles A. Lockwood thereafter). What happened when a submarine engaged a carrier in real warfare? Usually anticlimax. Sometimes, though, the event lived up to the legend, not least ten times in the Pacific Ocean.

The wardroom of a USN fleet submarine during a meal. This photograph predates the United States' entry into World War II. The fancy china and cutlery and the formal dress pictured here did not feature during war patrols. (AC)

CHRONOLOGY

1941
December 7 Japan attacks Pearl Harbor. The attacking fleet includes the aircraft carriers *Kaga* and *Shōkaku*.

1942
May 8–21 Nine USN submarines unsuccessfully attempt to intercept and attack the damaged carriers *Shōkaku* and *Zuikaku*.

June 4 *Nautilus* attacks *Kaga* during the battle of Midway and scores a hit, but the torpedo is a dud.

September 28 *Trout* intercepts *Taiyō* and fires five torpedoes; one hits but the others miss or prematurely explode. *Taiyō* is the first Japanese carrier damaged by a USN submarine.

December 17 *Drum* attacks *Ryūhō* off Bungo Suido, and hits it with one torpedo out of four fired. The damaged carrier reaches port and is repaired.

1943
April 8 *Tunny* intercepts *Hiyō*, *Jun'yō*, and *Taiyō*, and fires ten torpedoes at all three. *Taiyō* is damaged by one hit, while torpedoes fired at *Jun'yō* prematurely explode.

June 10 *Trigger* fires six torpedoes at *Hiyō* off Tokyo Bay; two miss, two prematurely explode, and two hit with one a dud.

December 4 *Sailfish* sinks *Chūyō* off Yokosuka. *Chūyō* is the first Japanese aircraft carrier sunk by a USN submarine.

1944
January 12 *Hake* sinks the IJA aircraft carrier/transport *Nigitsu Maru* off Okino-Daito Island in the South China Sea.

January 19 *Haddock* attacks *Shōkaku* in a Japanese task force off the Marianas. The torpedoes miss *Shōkaku*, but two hit and badly damage *Un'yō*.

June 19 *Albacore* sinks *Taihō* and *Cavalla* sinks *Shōkaku* during the battle of the Philippine Sea.

August 18 Off the coast of Luzon near the Luzon Strait, *Rasher* sinks *Taiyō*.

September 16 *Barb* attacks and sinks *Un'yō* near Hong Kong in the South China Sea.

November 3 *Pintado* launches torpedoes at *Jun'yō* near Makung in the South China Sea. The torpedoes are spotted by the destroyer *Akikaze*, which deliberately sails into them. *Akikaze* is sunk but *Jun'yō* is unharmed.

November 15 *Queenfish* torpedoes and sinks the IJA aircraft carrier/transport *Akitsu Maru* off Kyūshū in the Korean Strait.

November 17 While escorting a convoy in the South China Sea, *Shin'yō* is attacked and sunk by *Spadefish*.

November 29 *Archerfish* spots *Shinano* leaving Tokyo Bay, tracks it down and torpedoes it. *Shinano* sinks before reaching port.

December 8–9 *Sea Devil* and *Redfish* make separate attacks on *Jun'yō*. *Sea Devil* damages the carrier and *Redfish* reduces it to a total constructive loss.

December 19 *Redfish* sinks *Unryū* off Shanghai. *Unryū* is the last carrier sunk by a USN submarine.

December 28 *Dace* makes an attack on an unidentified Japanese carrier in the South China Sea. Three torpedoes are fired; all miss. It is the last attack on a Japanese carrier by a USN submarine in World War II.

THE STRATEGIC SITUATION

The duels between USN fleet submarines and Japanese aircraft carriers were children of the naval limitations treaties of the 1920s and 1930s. These treaties set Japan on the course that resulted in World War II's Pacific War (December 7, 1941–September 2, 1945); and they defined the two types of vessels that participated in these actions both in terms of design and function.

World War I was triggered in part by a naval armaments race between Britain and Germany. The appearance of the dreadnought battleship provided a moment in naval history that leveled all navies. The dreadnought eliminated secondary armament larger than that capable of dealing with torpedo boats; and it replaced the multiple gun sizes aboard previous battleships with a single battery of the largest-caliber guns.

Dreadnoughts rendered all previous battleships obsolete. Germany's leader, Kaiser Wilhelm II, decided Germany needed a powerful navy to achieve its place in the sun. The dreadnought offered Germany an opportunity to match the strength of Britain's Royal Navy. The United States, France, Russia, Italy, and Japan soon joined the dreadnought race. Even some South American countries had their own dreadnought rivalry.

Except for the United States no country, not even Germany, could match Britain's shipbuilding capability. Britain's shipbuilding industry also produced dreadnoughts for other countries, including Brazil, Chile, Japan, Spain, and the Ottoman Empire. Countries with lesser industrial capability, such as France, Italy, and Russia, scaled their dreadnought construction to match their economies – but not Japan. Starting in 1907 its Naval Staff began an ambitious program to increase the country's shipbuilding capability and dreadnought fleet, known as the Eight-Eight Fleet. Japan viewed the United States (with which it then had no fundamental disagreement) as its presumed enemy to justify construction of a fleet of eight dreadnought battleships and eight armored cruisers. (Eight battlecruisers were later substituted for the armored cruisers.) The fiscal expenditure required to undertake this shipbuilding program would have doubled Japan's national budget for all purposes.

Under the terms of the Washington Naval Treaty, countries could convert two dreadnoughts to aircraft carriers. Japan chose to convert two Amagi-class battlecruisers, including *Akagi*, shown here under construction at Kure Naval Arsenal. (Kure City Maritime History and Science Museum/ Wikimedia/Public Domain)

After World War I ended, Japan persisted with the Eight-Eight Fleet scheme; but warship growth required new ships to be designed and built if Japan was to achieve its goal of naval superiority. Only four battleships and four battlecruisers of the original Eight-Eight Fleet had been completed or were awaiting completion by then. The new program required construction of another 16 dreadnoughts, all with 16in main batteries. It would have bankrupted Japan.

France and Italy dropped out of the dreadnought race during World War I; and Russia dropped into the chaos of the Russian Revolution. Britain and the United States accelerated their shipbuilding programs. Britain completed ten battleships and two battlecruisers during World War I, and had another four battlecruisers under construction at war's end. All were armed with 15in main batteries.

The United States completed six battleships armed with 14in main batteries during World War I, and had another seven under construction, four of which were to carry 16in main batteries. By 1920 keels were being laid for an additional six battleships and six battlecruisers, all to be armed with 16in main batteries. Japan's Eight-Eight Fleet plans triggered this postwar battleship construction spree. By making the United States its notional enemy, Japan succeeded in turning the United States from a friendly neutral into a wary adversary motivated to develop a fleet capable of fighting across the greater distances of the Pacific Ocean rather than the Atlantic Ocean.

If the United States continued its dreadnought program, Britain had to increase its own dreadnought production to maintain parity. Both countries were reluctant to spend massive amounts building and operating warships, however, preferring to allocate spending to meet domestic needs and paying down war debt. Naval expansion was unpopular in the United States due to its cost. Consequently, President Warren G. Harding initiated naval limitations talks starting November 1921 in Washington, DC, and invited delegations from Britain, Japan, Italy, and France to attend.

The Washington Naval Treaty (also known as the Five-Power Treaty) was signed on February 6, 1922, and saved Japan from itself. The treaty limited the United States and Britain to 15 dreadnoughts, Japan to ten, and Italy and France to six each; limited the aggregate tonnage of battleships and aircraft carriers each navy could have along the same ratio; and forbade construction of new battleships (except two for Britain) until 1936. Furthermore, it limited the size and armament of ships that could be built while the treaty was in force. No warships (except aircraft carriers) exceeding 10,000 tons displacement and carrying guns in excess of 8in (203mm) diameter could be built. Aircraft carriers were defined as warships in excess of 10,000 tons standard displacement designed exclusively for carrying aircraft that could launch from and land on them; and they could not carry guns larger than 8in diameter.

The treaty excluded existing aircraft carriers from its provisions, however, ruling them to be experimental. It also permitted Britain, the United States, and Japan to convert two dreadnoughts each to aircraft carriers. All three countries took advantage of this provision. Britain converted the battlecruisers *Courageous* and *Glorious*, while the United States and Japan each selected two battlecruisers then under construction (*Lexington* and *Saratoga*; *Amagi* and *Akagi*) for conversion.

The treaty also barred construction of new Pacific fortifications, further increasing the Japanese and US navies' interest in long-range warships. Japan had no fortified bases outside Japan and Formosa; and the only fortified US bases were in the Philippines (viewed as untenable) and Hawaii. Both countries needed to project power roughly 4,000NM. They began designing warships with unrefueled ranges of 8,000NM.

The Washington Naval Treaty stopped the dreadnought race; but because it did not limit warship numbers for vessels under 10,000 tons displacement, it spurred building races in every other warship category. Cruisers immediately grew in size, coming in just under 10,000 tons with 8in main batteries. (In World War I light cruisers averaged 6,000 tons and carried 4–6in main batteries.) Japan built super-destroyers that reached 2,000 tons displacement, their main batteries equal in size to those of pre-World War I light cruisers. All the countries covered by the treaty's limitations built "cruiser" submarines carrying 6in or 8in deck guns and displacing as much as 3,250 tons surfaced.

A naval limitations conference was convened in London in April 1930 to discuss these excesses. It yielded the London Naval Treaty, signed on October 27, 1930, which subjected cruisers, destroyers, and submarines to individual and aggregate tonnage limitations similar to those for capital ships and aircraft carriers. It also limited the maximum size of guns that could be mounted on destroyers and submarines to 5.1in (129.5mm). Cruisers were divided into two categories: those carrying guns greater than 6.1in (155mm) and those carrying guns under that size. It also eliminated the 10,000-ton minimum standard displacement for future aircraft carriers, to prevent countries from evading carrier tonnage limitations with small carriers.

The treaty also required submarines to conform to the same international rules of war followed by surface warships. They could not sink a merchant ship or render it incapable of navigation unless those aboard the ship could be placed in a position of safety – and an open boat was not considered a position of safety in the open ocean. This rendered submarines incapable of commerce raiding.

The USN thereafter designed its submarines to fight warships in coordination with its surface fleet. This required submarines with large torpedo batteries (four torpedo hits were believed necessary to sink a capital ship), high surface speed, and extremely long range. These "fleet submarines" were intended to act against high-value naval targets: battleships, aircraft carriers, and large cruisers. They were also supposed to scout ahead of the fleet to provide early warning of the enemy's approach.

The Washington and London treaties further embittered Japan, which felt demeaned by the terms. It evaded and violated the terms whenever possible, before finally withdrawing from them in 1936. In turn, these actions alarmed the United States, which reacted by beginning to rearm. This further soured Japanese–US relations, which resulted in Japan launching a pre-emptive attack on Pearl Harbor on December 7, 1941. Three years and eight months of war ensued.

OPPOSITE

This map shows the area where encounters occurred between USN fleet submarines and Japanese aircraft carriers. It shows all the encounters in which Japanese carriers were sunk or damaged.

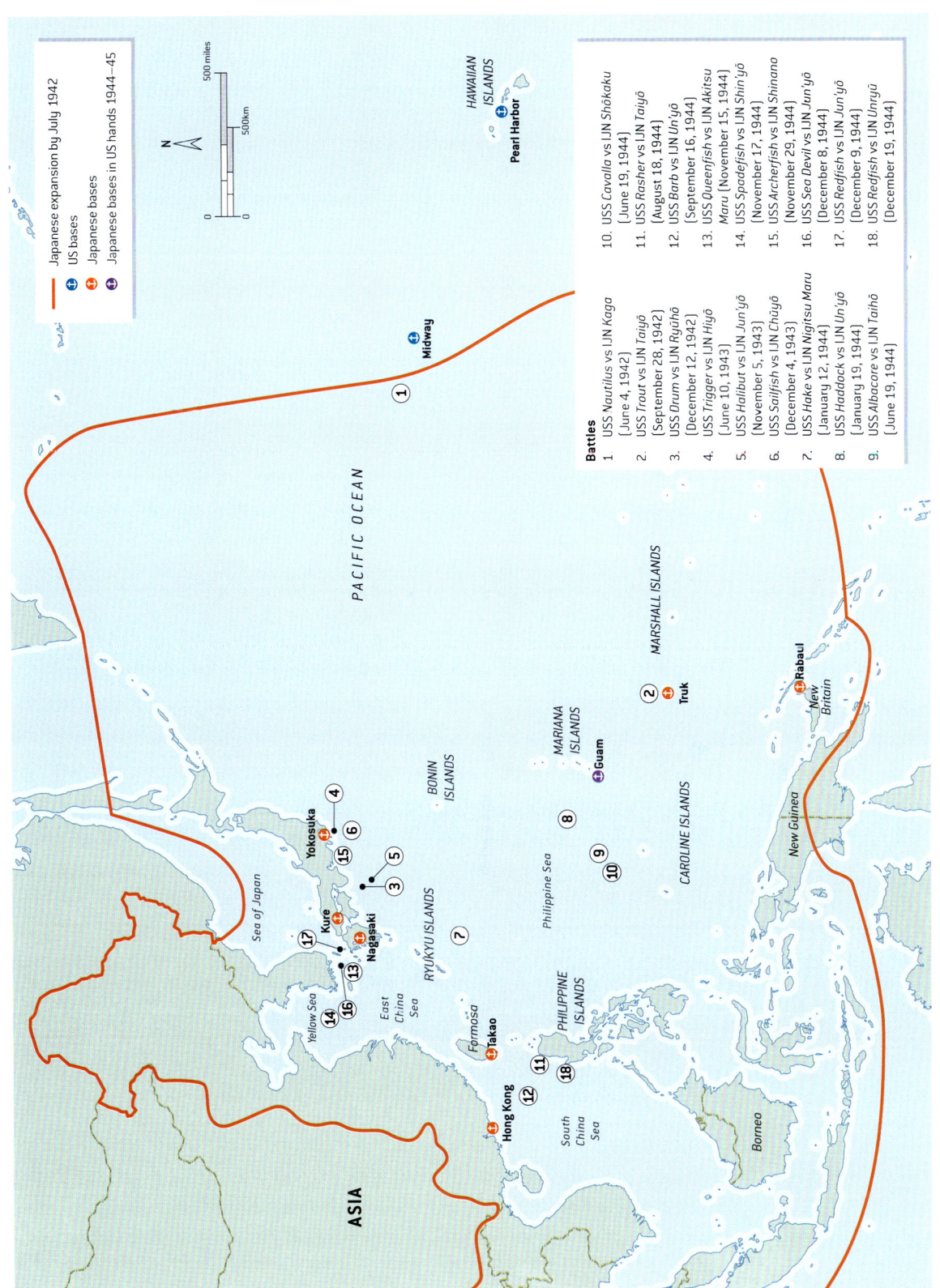

Japanese expansion by July 1942
US bases
Japanese bases
Japanese bases in US hands 1944–45

500 miles
500km

N

HAWAIIAN ISLANDS
Pearl Harbor

Midway

PACIFIC OCEAN

MARSHALL ISLANDS

Truk

Rabaul
New Britain

MARIANA ISLANDS
Guam

BONIN ISLANDS

CAROLINE ISLANDS

New Guinea

Yokosuka
Kure
Nagasaki

Sea of Japan

RYUKYU ISLANDS

Philippine Sea

East China Sea
Yellow Sea

Formosa
Takao

PHILIPPINE ISLANDS

Hong Kong

South China Sea

Borneo

ASIA

Battles

1. USS *Nautilus* vs IJN *Kaga* (June 4, 1942)
2. USS *Trout* vs IJN *Taiyō* (September 28, 1942)
3. USS *Drum* vs IJN *Ryūhō* (December 12, 1942)
4. USS *Trigger* vs IJN *Hiyō* (June 10, 1943)
5. USS *Halibut* vs IJN *Jun'yō* (November 5, 1943)
6. USS *Sailfish* vs IJN *Chūyō* (December 4, 1943)
7. USS *Hake* vs IJN *Nigitsu Maru* (January 12, 1944)
8. USS *Haddock* vs IJN *Un'yō* (January 19, 1944)
9. USS *Albacore* vs IJN *Taihō* (June 19, 1944)
10. USS *Cavalla* vs IJN *Shōkaku* (June 19, 1944)
11. USS *Rasher* vs IJN *Taiyō* (August 18, 1944)
12. USS *Barb* vs IJN *Un'yō* (September 16, 1944)
13. USS *Queenfish* vs IJN *Akitsu Maru* (November 15, 1944)
14. USS *Spadefish* vs IJN *Shin'yō* (November 17, 1944)
15. USS *Archerfish* vs IJN *Shinano* (November 29, 1944)
16. USS *Sea Devil* vs IJN *Jun'yō* (December 8, 1944)
17. USS *Redfish* vs IJN *Un'yō* (December 9, 1944)
18. USS *Redfish* vs IJN *Unryū* (December 19, 1944)

DESIGN AND DEVELOPMENT

Combat between submarines and aircraft carriers – profoundly different vessels – defined asymmetrical warfare. Through the first half of the 20th century, submarines operated individually, in isolation from the fleet. They were relatively lightly armed. Torpedoes were powerful, but submarines carried relatively few of them and could launch fewer simultaneously. Aircraft carriers were mobile airfields. The bigger they were the more aircraft they could carry and the longer the "runway." They were always part of a task force; and they had tremendous offensive power, carrying up to 100 aircraft.

Both, however, were highly vulnerable to attack. A submarine had little reserve buoyancy, which meant the loss of a single compartment could sink it. Carriers were filled with volatile fuel and explosive aircraft weapons. Both vessels were complex, and most successful when striking the first blow. They made a curiously balanced match.

THE USN FLEET SUBMARINE

The submarine powered by an internal combustion engine while surfaced and an electric motor while submerged, was developed in the United States. John P. Holland built his first submarine in 1878. The USN purchased Holland's most advanced design (*Holland VI*) in 1900, becoming the world's first navy to commission a submarine.

The USN was enthusiastic about submarines, viewing them as a tool to protect the US coast when the battle line was elsewhere. Between 1900 and the start of World

War I in August 1914 the USN commissioned over 30 submarines. During that period they evolved. Periscopes and multiple torpedo tubes arrived in 1905. (Before the advent of periscopes, submarines had to repeatedly surface and dive to aim their torpedoes. This behavior was similar to that of dolphins – "sea pigs" – leading USN submariners to dub their vessels "pig boats.")

By 1914 USN submarines typically had four bow torpedo tubes, were 135–161ft long, had double hulls, displaced 340–400 tons (surfaced), could travel 2,500–3,500NM cruising at 8–11kn, and had a test depth of 200ft. Diesel engines replaced those powered by gasoline. Radios were standard equipment, although aerials were erected only after surfacing.

World War I revealed the submarine's potential – Germany nearly defeated Britain with its U-boat campaign – which served to increase the USN's interest in its capabilities. The USN had laid down 47 submarines between 1900 and August 1914, 31 of which were commissioned and 16 under construction when the war started. The USN started construction of 29 submarines between August 1914 and the United States' entry into the war in April 1917.

During the 20 months the United States was a belligerent (April 1917–November 1918), it started construction of another 56 submarines. Contracts for a further 26 were placed. These wartime-built O, R, and S classes saw service in both World Wars. Primarily used for training in World War II, the O and R classes were designed prior to the United States' entry into World War I and represented prewar thinking about how best to use submarines. They were intended for coastal defense – a cheap way to attack capital ships approaching North America in the absence of the USN's battle fleet. (The USN was at that time a one-ocean force.)

The O-class boats (16 built) were the first in the USN to have deck guns. The guns made them a threat to ships deemed too small for torpedo attack, thus allowing the boats to be used as commerce raiders. They were larger than previous submarines, 172–186ft in length with displacements 50 percent to twice as large as earlier USN submarines. Their range was 3,700–4,700NM. While keeping the four bow torpedo tubes of earlier designs, the R-class boats (27 built) carried 21in torpedo tubes, which became standard for all future USN submarines.

OVERLEAF

The Narwhal and Sargo classes were built before World War II. *Nautilus* was one of the V-boats; designed before the 1922 Washington Naval Treaty limitations were imposed, there were no restrictions on their design. Intended as commerce raiders, they had heavy deck-gun armament. *Sailfish* of the Sargo class was representative of the USN's fleet submarines built after the 1930 London Naval Treaty.

NAUTILUS (NARWHAL CLASS)

Displacement   2,730 tons (surfaced); 3,900 tons (submerged)

Dimensions   371ft (overall) × 33ft 3in × 16ft 11in

Test depth   300ft

Propulsion   Two 2,350bhp and two 450bhp diesel engines (surface); two 800bhp electric motors (submerged)

Speed   17kn (surfaced); 8kn (submerged)

Endurance   9,380NM at 10kn or 25,000NM at 5.7kn (surfaced); 10hrs at 5kn (submerged)

Fuel   Diesel

Crew (1942)   Nine officers, 88 enlisted

Armament (1942)   Two (2×1) 6in/53 guns; four 0.50 machine guns; ten 21in torpedo tubes (four forward internal, two aft internal, two forward external, two aft external); up to 38 torpedoes (26 internal, 8–12 external)

SAILFISH (SARGO CLASS)

Displacement	1,450 tons (surfaced); 2,415 tons (submerged)
Dimensions	310ft 6in (overall) × 26ft 10in × 16ft 8in
Test depth	250ft
Propulsion	Four 1,535bhp diesel engines (surface); four 685bhp electric motors
Speed	21kn (surfaced); 8.75kn (submerged)
Endurance	11,000NM at 10kn (surfaced); 48hrs at 2kn (submerged)
Fuel	Diesel
Crew	5 officers, 54 enlisted
Armament	One 3in/50 gun; two (2x1) 20mm/70 antiaircraft guns; eight 21in torpedo tubes (four forward, four aft)*; 24 21in torpedoes

* Some Sargo-class boats were fitted with two external torpedo tubes forward

The S-class boats (51 built) marked an even more significant change. Displacing 1,000–1,200 tons surfaced, they could travel up to 5,900NM on internal fuel and up to 10,000NM using fuel carried in the main ballast tanks. (This created problems, however. Until the ballast tanks were scrubbed, residual oil created oil slicks, which revealed a submarine's presence.) They carried a 4in deck gun (previous classes had 3in guns) and were intended to fight in the Atlantic, projecting power far from the United States' Atlantic coast.

After World War I the USN realized its most probable future foe was Japan. The next war would likely involve fighting in the Pacific, for which the S-class boats were too small and lacking in range and duration. The USN responded by designing the V-class boats (nine built) for a Pacific War. Rather than a single design the V class consisted of five different designs to determine what would be the configuration of the standard USN submarine going forward. They were the only USN submarines built between 1921 and 1934.

V-1 through *V-3*, started in 1921, were intended as fleet submarines, capable of operating with the USN's battle fleet. They displaced 2,119 tons surfaced and were 342ft long; the largest submarines built to date for the USN. They had six torpedo tubes, four forward and two aft (a first), a 6,000NM range (11,000NM using fuel carried in the ballast tanks), two direct-drive diesel engines for surface propulsion and two others to charge the batteries for the electric motors.

The design was a failure. Intended to make 21kn surfaced, the trio achieved 18.7kn. They were poor sea boats and too heavy forward. Commissioned in 1924 and 1925, they were renamed *Barracuda*, *Bass*, and *Bonita* in 1931. Decommissioned in 1937, they were recommissioned when World War II started but discarded in 1943.

The next three, *V-4* through *V-6*, were larger still. *V-4* (renamed *Argonaut*) displaced 3,046 tons and was 381ft long. The USN's sole minelaying submarine, it had four forward torpedo tubes and two aft mine tubes with 60 mines. *V-5* and *V-6* (later *Narwhal* and *Nautilus*) were oceangoing "cruiser" submarines. They displaced 2,730 tons surfaced and were 371ft long. Four torpedo tubes were located forward and two aft. Built using welding, all three had a test depth of 300ft and carried two 6in deck guns.

Argonaut's surface speed topped at 15kn; it could travel 8,000NM at 10kn. *Narwhal* and *Nautilus* could reach 17kn and 9,380NM at 10kn. (Their range increased to 18,000NM and 25,000NM respectively using fuel carried in the ballast tanks.) They used direct-drive diesel engines for surface travel. All three were a design dead-end, too unwieldy for standard submarine operations.

The fourth V-boat design, *Dolphin*, was both lighter and smaller at 1,718 tons and 319ft long. It made 18kn surfaced, had a range of 4,900NM on internal fuel (18,780NM using fuel carried in the ballast tanks), and a test depth of 300ft. It had the same torpedo-tube arrangement as the Narwhals, but only one 4in deck gun. The follow-on Cachalot-class boats, *Cachalot* and *Cuttlefish*, displaced 1,110 tons and were 274ft long. Retrograde features were a test depth of only 250ft and a single 3in deck gun.

Six subsequent classes of USN submarines, from the Porpoise through Sargo classes, followed this basic design. They were larger than the Cachalots, with displacements varying from 1,310 to 1,450 tons and measuring 298–310ft long. Beginning with the Porpoise class (ten built) they had dramatically longer range – 11,000NM on internal fuel; long enough for war patrols off Japan from bases in Hawaii.

The subsequent Salmon (six built) and Sargo (ten built) classes increased the number of stern-mounted torpedo tubes to four, and carried 24 torpedoes compared to the previous classes' 16. The real change, however, was internal, for these boats were designed to take advantage of improvements in torpedo fire control and sonar. They also used new lightweight diesel engines, increasing the power and reliability of these boats' propulsion.

By the end of World War I US torpedoes could change course up to 90 degrees after launch by setting gyros, meaning USN submarines no longer had to aim directly at a target. Determining the gyro angle involved complex computations, however. The Bureau of Ordnance developed a torpedo data computer (TDC) for the necessary calculations, installing it on these fleet submarines. By 1930 the Bureau of Ordnance had developed passive sonars to further aid targeting.

The 1930s saw the introduction of new 1,300–1,600bhp mass-produced, lightweight diesel-electric engines, which debuted in *Porpoise*. By World War II, 1,600bhp diesel engines manufactured by General Motors and Fairbanks-Morse were standard. They drove generators powering electric motors that turned the propellers.

The Tambor class (12 built) represented the arrival of the standard Pacific War fleet submarine. The design had ten torpedo tubes – six forward, four aft – to facilitate attacks against capital ships. USN designers felt the potential to launch six torpedoes offered a better chance to sink large warships, allowing a margin for misses. Gun mounts fore and aft were capable of carrying a 5in deck gun. Below deck they were equipped with air conditioning, cold storage, showers, and fresh-water distillers, significantly improving long-mission liveability. Multiple sonars were installed, improving direction-finding and ranging capabilities. The conning tower was enlarged and the TDC and sonar operators relocated there, effectively creating a Combat Information Center (CIC) within it.

The follow-on Gato class (77 built) was an improved Tambor, 5ft longer to allow a bulkhead splitting the single engine room of the Tambors into two smaller engine rooms to increase survivability. The design had a test depth of 300ft. A negative buoyancy tank was added to speed diving, allowing the boats to submerge in 60 seconds. During the war, holes were drilled in the outer hull to allow water to fill faster when diving. Boats with these limber holes could submerge in 30 seconds.

The Balao class (120 built), the ultimate World War II USN fleet submarine, incorporated further improvements based on wartime experience. The hull was thicker and used high-tensile steel, resulting in a test depth of 400ft. The sail (the unpressurized superstructure above the conning tower) was reduced to minimize the profile when on the surface. They were also designed for radar, which was retrofitted into earlier submarines.

OVERLEAF

The wartime-built Gato and Balao classes were both developments of the Tambor class. The biggest difference between the two classes was the Balaos had a thicker hull than the Gatos, made of high-tensile steel. The result was Balaos had a deeper test depth. In reality many Gato skippers safely took their boats 450ft deep, while at least one Balao skipper (Lieutenant Commander Richard H. O'Kane of *Tang*) took his boat down to 600ft.

ALBACORE (GATO CLASS)

Displacement	1,526 tons (surfaced); 2,410 tons (submerged)
Dimensions	311ft 9in (overall) × 27ft 3in × 15ft 3in
Test depth	300ft
Propulsion	Four 1,350bhp diesel engines (surface); four 685bhp electric motors
Speed	21kn (surfaced); 8.75kn (submerged)
Endurance	11,000NM at 10kn (surfaced); 48hrs at 2kn (submerged)
Fuel	Diesel
Crew	Six officers, 54 enlisted
Armament (1944)	One 3in/50 gun; one 20mm/70 antiaircraft gun; ten 21in torpedo tubes (six forward, four aft); 24 21in torpedoes

ARCHERFISH (BALAO CLASS)

Displacement	1,525 tons (surfaced); 2,415 tons (submerged)
Dimensions	311ft 9in (overall) × 27ft 3in × 15ft 3in
Test depth	400ft
Propulsion	Four 1,350bhp diesel engines (surface); four 685bhp electric motors
Speed	20.25kn (surfaced); 8.75kn (submerged)
Endurance	11,000NM at 10kn (surfaced); 48hrs at 2kn (submerged)
Fuel	Diesel
Crew	Ten officers, 71 enlisted
Armament	One or two 5in/25 guns; various 20mm and 40mm antiaircraft guns; ten 21in torpedo tubes (six forward, four aft); 24 21in torpedoes

THE IJN AIRCRAFT CARRIER

The IJN adopted naval aviation early. Its first aircraft carrier, a converted merchantman capable of operating four seaplanes, was commissioned prior to the outbreak of World War I as the naval auxiliary *Wakamiya Maru*. It was the first carrier to use aircraft in combat, raiding German-held Tsingtao in September 1914.

In December 1919 Japan laid the keel for its first true aircraft carrier, *Hōshō*. Although it was the first aircraft carrier designed from the keel up to carry, launch, and land aircraft, it was an adaptation of a fast fleet oiler design. (It was commissioned on December 27, 1922, a year before Britain's first keel-up carrier, *Hermes*, laid-down in 1918, but left incomplete until 1923.) *Hōshō* had a full-length (541ft×70ft) flight deck with the funnels for the boilers trunked over the starboard side. As built, it had a small island starboard, forward of the funnels.

Hōshō was small; 7,590 tons and 551ft long. It had a top speed of 25kn, and could steam 8,000NM unrefueled at 10kn. It carried 26 aircraft. A pioneering design, it was the last keel-up aircraft carrier built by Japan for ten years and was superior to the first carriers commissioned for the Royal and US navies, *Argus* and *Langley* respectively, which were conversions of an ocean liner and collier respectively.

The IJN's next two carriers were dreadnought conversions. The Washington Naval Treaty forced Japan to scrap or cancel the two Amagi-class battlecruisers (*Amagi* and *Akagi*) and the two Tosa-class battleships (*Tosa*, launched on December 18, 1921, and *Kaga*). The treaty allowed signatories to convert two ships under construction and which would otherwise be scrapped to aircraft carriers. The ships chosen had to be less than 33,000 tons; their tonnage counted toward treaty aircraft carrier tonnage limitations.

Japan selected *Amagi* and *Akagi* for conversion. They displaced a reported 30,000 tons (in actuality, 36,500 tons), were 770ft long at the waterline, had a top speed of 32.5kn, and could steam 8,000NM at 14kn. On September 1, 1923, however, the Great Kantō Earthquake wrecked *Amagi*, under construction at Yokosuka Naval Arsenal. *Kaga*, then incomplete and awaiting scrapping, replaced *Amagi*. *Kaga*, even bigger than *Akagi*, displaced less (29,600 tons) according to official reports.

Hōshō was the first aircraft carrier built for the IJN, and the first to be commissioned anywhere in the world that was designed from the outset as a carrier rather than being a conversion. Although superseded by later carriers, when *Hōshō* was commissioned on December 27, 1922, it was the world's best aircraft carrier. (Kure City Maritime History and Science Museum /Wikimedia/Public Domain)

Sōryū was the last Japanese carrier built to naval treaty tonnage limitations. Although 1,000 tons heavier than *Hiryū*, *Sōryū* also suffered from poor internal protection, structural weakness, and stability issues. (Kure City Maritime History and Science Museum/Wikimedia/ Public Domain)

It had a waterline length of 754ft 7in, breadth of 97ft, drew 26ft, and actually displaced 38,200 tons. It had a top speed of 28kn, and could steam 10,000NM at 15kn.

Akagi and *Kaga* were built as aircraft carriers with three flight decks, theoretically allowing simultaneous multiple-deck aircraft launches. Each carried 60 aircraft, but neither initially had islands. Both initially carried ten 200mm (7.9in) guns and 12 120mm (4.7in) antiaircraft guns in twin mounts. Each had a 152mm (6in) armor belt. *Akagi* carried 79mm (3.1in) of deck armor; *Kaga* had 38mm (1.5in). Except for the USN's Lexington class, they were the most powerful aircraft carriers in the world when commissioned on March 25, 1927, and November 30, 1929, respectively. They remained the largest aircraft carriers Japan built until *Shinano*.

They were not completely satisfactory aircraft carriers, however. Internal arrangements below the main deck were little changed from their dreadnought design. Boiler uptakes were trunked to the starboard side. Magazines for 410mm (16in) shells were modified to hold bombs and torpedoes. The hangar was built above the main deck (with a flying-off deck on the forward third of the main deck), with the two flight decks atop the hangar. Two elevators took aircraft between the hangar deck and flight decks.

Both carriers were extensively rebuilt in the mid-1930s. Multiple flight decks were replaced with a single ship-length flight deck. *Akagi* gained an island to port; *Kaga* got one to starboard. Bomb and torpedo elevators were modified to send munitions to the flight deck. The boilers were changed from a coal/oil mix to exclusively oil-fired boilers. Aircraft capacity was increased to 90 (72 ready, 18 in reserve). The 120mm antiaircraft guns were replaced with 127mm (5in) guns and 25mm (1in) light antiaircraft guns were added.

Japan designed only two more carriers while under naval limitations treaties. Carrier tonnage available under the Washington Naval Treaty resulted in a pair of near-sister ships, *Sōryū* and *Hiryū*. Rated at 16,200 tons, *Sōryū*, commissioned on December 29, 1937, filled out the remaining treaty tonnage allowance. *Hiryū*,

OVERLEAF

Kaga and *Shinano* both started out as battleships, but were converted to aircraft carriers during construction. As a result both were the IJN's most heavily armored carriers. Initially intended as artillery platforms, their internal hull arrangements were designed around turrets and magazines for large guns. Facilities for aircraft were located above the upper hull deck, which resulted in both carriers having towering superstructures. *Shinano* had a pink flight deck when sunk, due to an unpainted shock-absorbing deck layer composed of latex and red cedar sawdust. The green-and-pink carrier may have had the most unusual appearance of any carrier in World War II.

KAGA

Displacement	38,200 tons
Dimensions	247.65m (812ft 6in) × 32.5m (106ft 8in) × 9.48m (31ft 1in)
Propulsion	Eight Kampon water-tube boilers, 127,400shp (95,000kW); four geared steam turbines; four shafts
Speed	28kn
Fuel	Fuel oil
Range	19,000km (10,259NM) at 15kn
Crew	1,708
Armor	152mm (6in) belt; 38mm (1.5in) deck
Armament (1942)	Ten (10×1) 200mm (7.9in) guns; 16 (8×2) 127mm (5in) dual-purpose guns; 22 (11×2) 25mm (1in) Type 96 antiaircraft guns; 90 aircraft

SHINANO

Displacement	73,040 tons
Dimensions	265.8m (872ft 2in) × 36.3m (131ft) × 10.3m (33ft 10in)
Propulsion	12 Kampon water-tube boilers, 150,000shp (110,000kW); four geared steam turbines; four shafts
Speed	27kn
Fuel	Fuel oil
Range	19,000km (10,259NM) at 18kn
Crew	2,400
Armor	160–400mm (6.3–15.75in) belt; 115mm (4.53in) main deck, 75mm (3in) flight deck
Armament (1944)	16 (8×2) 127mm (5in) dual-purpose guns; 135 (45×3) 25mm (1in) Type 96 antiaircraft guns; 336 (12×28) 120mm (4.7in) antiaircraft rocket launchers; 45 aircraft

1,000 tons greater and commissioned on July 5, 1939, was ordered after Japan decided to withdraw from all naval limitations treaties in January 1936.

Both carriers suffered from Washington Naval Treaty tonnage limitations, and proved to be unsatisfactory. To save weight they had no protection. *Sōryū*, with its island to starboard ahead of the funnels, had stability problems (partially corrected in *Hiryū* by increasing tonnage and placing the island to port, opposite the funnel uptakes). Both could carry 72 aircraft (63 ready, nine in reserve). With a top speed of 34kn, they had a Pacific-spanning range of 7,750NM at 18kn.

The two Shōkaku-class aircraft carriers, *Shōkaku* and *Zuikaku*, designed after Japan's withdrawal from all naval limitations treaties, proved the first completely satisfactory IJN carrier design. They displaced 32,105 tons, could reach 34.5kn, and cruise 9,700NM at 18kn. They also had elaborate internal protection through compartmentalization, and were armored: their waterline belt was 46–165mm and their deck armor, which was on the main deck, was 45–132mm. Flight and hangar decks were unarmored. They also had heavy antiaircraft protection, being initially armed with 16 127mm (5in) guns in twin mounts and 36 25mm (1in) light antiaircraft guns in triple mounts. They carried 84 aircraft (72 ready, 12 in reserve), were superior to the USN's Yorktown class, and matched the wartime Essex class.

Japan would go on to produce two more classes of aircraft carriers during World War II: *Taihō*, an improved Shōkaku; and the two improved Sōryūs, *Unryū* and *Amagi*, of the Unryū class. *Taihō*, laid down on July 10, 1941, displaced 29,300 tons and was modified during construction to incorporate wartime lessons. It had underwater protection superior to the Shōkakus, and an armored flight deck, with 76mm armor intended to stop a 1,000lb bomb. It also had a 152mm armor belt. Armor protection accounted for 8,800 tons of its weight. It was designed to carry 12 100mm (3.9in) and 71 25mm (1in) antiaircraft guns. The bow was plated up to the flight deck, to improve seakeeping. Top speed was 33.33kn and it could steam 8,000NM at 18kn. It was the most formidable aircraft carrier Japan built.

Six Unryū-class carriers were laid down after the Pacific War started but only *Unryū* and *Amagi* were commissioned, both in August 1944. They displaced 17,480 tons,

Japan's fourth carrier, *Ryūjō*, exploited a loophole in the Washington Naval Treaty. At 9,910 tons, it did not "qualify" as an aircraft carrier under the treaty's tonnage limitations and so did not add to Japan's tonnage limit. It carried 48 aircraft, had a top speed of 29kn, and could steam 10,000NM at 14kn. Its light weight was achieved by sacrificing protection. Additionally, it was top-heavy. *Ryūjō* exemplified the futility of evading the terms of the Washington Naval Treaty by building carriers under 10,000 tons. The loophole was closed by the 1930 London Naval Treaty, which counted the tonnage of all fast warships (those with a top speed in excess of 20kn) against treaty tonnage limitations. (AC)

were 746ft long, could make 34kn, and steam 8,000NM at 18kn. They had no armor protection, and carried 60 aircraft each.

The IJN commissioned 16 other aircraft carriers during its existence. Of these, 14 were "shadow" carriers, built or designed as fast naval auxiliaries in such a way as to facilitate their conversion to aircraft carriers. Two other carriers were started as surface warships, but converted while under construction to carry aircraft.

To evade treaty tonnage limitations, Japan built fast naval auxiliaries – fleet oilers, seaplane tenders, submarine depot ships, and destroyer tenders (uncontrolled by treaty limitations) – which could be converted to aircraft carriers. Five, designed and laid down before Japan withdrew from the treaties, were actually finished as seaplane tenders or submarine depot ships. These became *Chitose*, *Chiyoda*, *Shōhō*, *Zuihō*, and *Ryūhō*. They displaced 11,000–13,000 tons, could make 26.5–29kn, steam 8,000NM at 18kn, carried 24–31 aircraft, and could operate in conjunction with the fleet carriers. They were also unarmored, with the internal compartmentalization of auxiliaries rather than warships, providing a lesser degree of damage control.

Seven of Japan's carriers were converted from fast passenger liners. They ranged from 13,000 to 24,000 tons and were capable of making 21–25kn. Most carried 21–27 aircraft, although *Hiyō* and *Jun'yō*, converted from fast passenger liners for the North American run, carried 53 and 42–48 respectively. The Imperial Japanese Army (IJA) converted *Akitsu Maru* and *Nigitsu Maru*, two 11,800-ton, 20kn troop transports, into aircraft carriers/transports capable of carrying 20 aircraft. All had the damage-control capabilities of merchant ships.

After the battle of Midway (June 4–7, 1942), Japan chose to convert two warships under construction to carriers: the Mogami-class heavy cruiser *Ibuki* and the Yamato-class battleship *Shinano*. *Ibuki* was never completed, but would have been analogous to US Independence-class light carriers. *Shinano* was never completed either. It was torpedoed and sunk by *Archerfish* on November 29, 1944, while steaming from Yokosuka, where it had been built, to Kure Naval Arsenal to be fitted out. It was a 73,040-ton monster, 872ft long and 131ft across, which could make 27kn and steam 10,000NM at 18kn. It retained its battleship belt armor of 160–400mm with a total of 190mm of deck armor (75mm on the flight deck and 115mm on the main deck).

Jun'yō was one of two Hiyō-class escort carriers converted from the fast passenger liners *Kashiwara Maru* and *Izumo Maru*. Both were acquired by the IJN in 1941 and entered service as escort carriers in 1942, part of Japan's "shadow" carrier program. (USNHHC)

OVERLEAF
The Shōkaku and Taihō classes were the most capable aircraft carriers produced for the IJN. Designed from the outset as carriers, they were optimized for operating aircraft. They were the best-protected Japanese carriers except for those originally intended to be battleships or battlecruisers. They also had heavy antiaircraft batteries, and were designed to carry 65–72 aircraft. *Shōkaku* was one of the first carriers equipped with radar, mounting a Type 13 air search radar in August 1942.

SHŌKAKU

Displacement	25,675 tons
Dimensions	257.5m (844ft 10in) × 26m (85ft 4in) × 8.8m (28ft 10in)
Propulsion	Eight Kampon RO-GO water-tube boilers, 160,000shp (120,000kW); four geared steam turbines; four shafts
Speed	33.33kn
Fuel	Fuel oil
Range	19,000km (10,259NM) at 18kn
Crew	1,600
Armor	150–215mm (5.9–8.5in) belt; 215mm (8.5in) deck
Armament (1944)	16 (8×2) 127mm (5in) dual-purpose guns; 70 (18×3, 16×1) 25mm (1in) Type 96 antiaircraft guns; 72 aircraft

TAIHŌ

Displacement	29,300 tons
Dimensions	260.6m (855ft) × 27.4m (89ft 11in) × 9.6m (31ft 6in)
Propulsion	Eight Kampon RO-GO water-tube boilers, 160,000shp (120,000kW); four geared steam turbines; four shafts
Speed	33.33kn
Fuel	Fuel oil
Range	14,800km (8,000NM) at 18kn
Crew	1,751
Armor	40–152mm (1.6–6in) belt; 40–80mm (1.3–3.1in) deck
Armament (1944)	12 (6×2) 100mm (3.9in) Type 98 antiaircraft guns; 51 (17×3) 25mm (1in) Type 96 antiaircraft guns; 65 aircraft

TECHNICAL
SPECIFICATIONS

USN FLEET SUBMARINE

The USN fleet submarine was a tool designed for sinking major enemy warships, including aircraft carriers. Everything about it – its range, its surface and submerged speed, the number of torpedo tubes it carried, its ability to submerge, and the depth to which it could submerge – was designed around that goal. The sensor suite it carried allowed it to detect a target while at a low risk of being discovered itself. The submarine depended on stealth and surprise for success. This section describes those characteristics.

STRUCTURE

The fleet submarine of World War II used double-hull construction. The inner hull was the pressure hull, which was a cylinder with hemispherical ends. It maintained a one-atmosphere internal pressure in which the crew lived and worked. The cylinder was penetrated by holes closed by sealed pressure hatches to permit entry and exit. These included crew hatches and pressure seals for the torpedo tubes. The pressure hull was divided into watertight compartments connected by hatches.

Starting with the V-boats, the fleet submarine had a two-part pressure hull. A second cylinder sat atop the main pressure hull, roughly amidships. This conning tower contained the equipment needed to conduct a torpedo attack, such as the periscopes, TDC, sonar room, and (when it appeared) radar room. It could be sealed from the main pressure hull by a watertight hatch.

The pressure hull defined the depth a submarine could dive, and was guaranteed to reach the test depth safely: 300ft for the V-boats and Gato class; 250ft for the Porpoise to Tambor classes; and 400ft for the Balao class. This was not particularly deep – German U-boats could dive 720ft – but the test depth was conservative. While never exceeded in peacetime, it was often exceeded during the war.

The outer hull was unpressurized; a shell providing streamlined flow through the water. The ballast tanks, which could be filled with air or water to allow a submarine to surface or dive respectively, were placed between the pressure and outer hull. The outer hull typically had a flat deck to improve crew access. Additionally, there was an outer shell around the conning tower, called the fairwater, to improve hydrodynamic flow and provide a platform for the bridge crew and antiaircraft guns.

Starting with *Argonaut*, the V-boats introduced welding that offered greater strength at lower weight than riveting. In *Argonaut* noncritical structure was welded. This included superstructure, pipe brackets, and support framing. The pressure hull, outer hull, ballast tanks, and internal framing were riveted or bolted. *Dolphin* saw increased welding, with portions of the outer hull, ballast tanks, and internal framing welded. With the Porpoise class, the five boats built by the USN in the Portsmouth Navy Yard, New Hampshire (*Porpoise*, *Pike*, *Plunger*, *Pollack*, and *Pompano*), followed the pattern set by *Argonaut*: riveting of the inner and outer hulls, and using welding on noncritical structure. The five boats built by the Electric Boat Company of Groton, New Hampshire (*Shark*, *Tarpon*, *Perch*, *Pickerel*, and *Permit*), were all-welded, as were all subsequent USN submarines built.

It took ten years for the USN to become comfortable with all-welded construction. Riveted construction was a known quantity, while welding was unfamiliar. Until welding quality could be guaranteed, especially at depth, the USN was unwilling to risk crews in all-welded submarines.

PROPULSION

All World War II submarines used a combination of diesel engines for surface propulsion and charging batteries and electric motors for underwater propulsion. In most navies, surface propulsion was achieved by connecting some or all of the diesels to the propellers using a clutch system while using those not driving the propellers to run a generator to charge batteries. Older USN submarines up to and including the V-class boats used direct-drive diesels for surface propulsion.

Subsequent classes used true diesel-electric propulsion, however, for which the diesels were connected to generators that either powered electric motors driving the propellers or charged the batteries. Electric current flowed to the motors based on available electricity. Diesel speed was independent of motor speed, allowing diesels to run at optimum speed. Speed became a function of current flow, controlled by a panel in the maneuvering room.

Diesel-electric was bulkier than direct drive, but it had many advantages. It allowed diesels to avoid critical speeds; and it permitted one or more diesels to be shut down for maintenance and overhaul without affecting propulsion. By drawing on batteries, submarines could make top surface speeds without overworking the diesels. Diesel-electric was quieter as the electric motors produced less noise than a laboring diesel and clutched gearing. Each submarine was driven by two propellers, turned by four high-speed electric motors connected to reduction gears.

The USN built their fleet submarines with four identical engines, allowing the submarine to run on any combination from 25 percent diesel power (one diesel) to 100 percent diesel power (four diesels). This required lightweight diesels that could produce 1bhp for every 15–30lb of engine weight. In the 1920s existing marine diesels typically yielded 1bhp for every 60lb of engine weight. The Bureau of Engineering sponsored the development of lightweight diesels.

By 1933, four US manufacturers were making lightweight diesels: Winton, Fairbanks-Morse, General Motors (GM), and Hoover, Owens Rentschler (HOR); but Winton and HOR had either production issues or reliability issues. As a consequence of this, the USN switched almost exclusively to Fairbanks-Morse and GM by the time the United States entered World War II. It went so far as to replace older engines supplied by other manufacturers (especially HOR) with Fairbanks-Morse and GM diesels when submarines went through refits. This included replacing the direct-diesel systems on the old V-boats with Fairbanks-Morse and GM diesels.

Fairbanks-Morse's two-stroke eight-cylinder diesels generated 1,600bhp. GM's two-stroke V-16 diesel also produced 1,600bhp. Both weighed 18lb/bhp; and both were highly reliable and easy to maintain. All moving parts except the crankshaft were light enough to replace quickly. The USN's fleet submarines now had reliable, robust, and fuel-efficient propulsion systems.

WEAPONRY

The only weapon a submarine carried that was effective against an aircraft carrier was the torpedo. During the period covered in this book, USN fleet submarines carried two types of torpedoes: the Mk 14 and Mk 18. Both had a 21in diameter and were 20ft 6in long.

The steam-powered Mk 14 was generally the torpedo used against aircraft carriers because it was faster and had a longer range. With two speed settings, it could travel 4,500yd at 46kn or 9,000yd at 31kn. It weighed 3,000lb, and carried a 507lb TNT or 668lb Torpex (torpedo explosive) warhead. It had wet-heater steam-turbine propulsion, which injected a mixture of compressed air, fuel, and water into a combustion chamber to produce steam to drive a turbine. The steam yielded a trail of

bubbles when it reached the surface. The Mk 14 entered service in 1931 and continued in use through World War II and into the 1970s.

Westinghouse Electric's Mk 18 adaptation of the German 21in G7e electric torpedo could travel just 4,000yd at 29kn, It weighed 3,041lb, and carried a 600lb Torpex warhead. Its main advantage over the Mk 14 torpedo was that it left no wake revealing its presence or pointing to the submarine that fired it. The Mk 18 entered service in 1944, but it proved to be temperamental in its initial year of use.

Both torpedoes used a Mk 12 Mod 3 gyro for guidance. The gyro kept the torpedo running straight, but it could also be set to change the direction of the torpedo after it left the torpedo tube by a preset angle (up to 90 degrees) from the direction of the torpedo tube. This ability permitted a spread of torpedoes to be launched along the length of the target, thus yielding a greater chance of successful hits. The TDC provided the angles, which were set before launching the torpedoes.

US torpedoes had smaller warheads than those of other navies, but the USN developed a magnetic exploder to overcome this limitation. Torpedoes would be set to run under the target ship, and the exploder, having detected the hull's magnetic influence, would explode under the keel, breaking it. The exploder and everything about it, including training manuals, were kept secret until the war started.

Inadequate training was initially thought to explain the exploder's failure. While training shortcomings contributed to its unreliability, the real problem was inadequate prewar testing of the design. Adequate testing would have shown the Earth's magnetic field affected the exploder's sensitivity when used in locations that were distant from where it was actually tested. US torpedoes had other flaws. They routinely ran deep, which meant that even if the exploder worked, the torpedo was too far below the target ship to explode; and warheads frequently prematurely exploded. Finally, the firing pin of the contact exploder was too weak and needed to be strengthened. Not until January 1944 were all the flaws fixed, allowing USN submarines to receive reliable torpedoes.

USN TORPEDOES

During the period covered in this book, USN fleet submarines used two types of 21in torpedoes against IJN aircraft carriers: the steam-powered Mk 14 and the electric Mk 18.

Designed in 1931, the Mk 14 (**1**) was developed and initially manufactured by the USN's Naval Torpedo Station (NTS) at Newport, Rhode Island. Owing to the failure of the NTS to develop an electric torpedo, development and manufacture of the Mk 18 (**2**) was undertaken by Westinghouse Electric. It was a copy of the German G7e torpedo. Whereas the NTS spent years developing the Mk 14 (and threatened to spend as long developing their version of the electric torpedo), Westinghouse Electric began development work in 1942 and had the Mk 18 in production by 1943.

US torpedo characteristics				
	Mk 14 Mod 0	**Mk 14 Mod 3**	**Mk 18 Mod 0**	**Mk 18 Mod 2**
Weight	3,000lb	3,061lb	3,041lb	3,061lb
Overall length/diameter	20ft 6in/21in			
Explosive charge	507lb TNT	668lb TPX	600lb TPX	595lb TPX or HBX
Range/speed	4,500yd at 46kn; 9,000yd at 31kn		4,000yd at 29kn	
Power	Wet-heater steam turbine		Electric battery	
Guidance	Mk 12 Mod 3 gyro			

SENSORS AND ELECTRONICS

The World War II fleet submarine had multiple means of detecting its targets, using observations taken from sonar, radar, periscope sightings, and visual observations by lookouts on deck. While many believe the majority of submarine attacks were carried out solely by means of visual observation, even in 1942 sonar attacks occurred; and by 1944 many successful attacks were carried out against targets unseen by visual observation.

Fleet submarines had two periscopes. In the older designs one periscope was in the conning tower, while the second was in the control room. The control room periscope was used for attack backup and general surface search. The wartime-built Gatos and Balaos had two periscopes (attack and search) in the conning tower. Periscopes had stadimeters, allowing them to be used for range finding.

The standard sonars on submarines in 1941 were called WCA and WDA. They operated at 18–24kHz, combining active and passive sonars and depth sounders. The bearing deviation indicator (BDI), introduced during the war, allowed submarines to track a target using sonar. Sonar range was generally more accurate than periscope range. Later in the war, sonar sets capable of torpedo and mine detection and object

In the popular view the periscope was the primary sensor used by submarines. In reality, while important, during World War II it was just one tool used to set up an attack. Skippers preferred to see the target being attacked. (USNHHC)

1	3" A.A. Moved For'd.
2	20% A.A. Gun
3	" Ready Serv. Bx.
6	Venturi Shield
7	Railing Altered
8	Radio Antenna
9	Underwater Loop Antenna
10	SD Radar Mast
11	SJ " "

A fleet submarine's radars were mounted on its radar mast, behind the night periscope. The SJ surface search radar's antenna is at the top of the mast (10) and the SD air search radar's antenna is the grid arc beneath the SJ antenna (11). (USNHHC)

location were installed. These were more useful for avoiding hazards than attacking targets.

The USN developed radar shortly before the United States entered World War II. The two types most commonly used aboard submarines were SD air search and SJ surface search. SD was introduced in 1941 and SJ in June 1942. Both operated on a 10cm wavelength.

By early 1943 all fleet submarines on combat patrol had radar. SD was omnidirectional, providing contact range, but not bearing. SJ was directional, providing both range and bearing. It could detect an aircraft carrier up to 12NM distant. Both types were mounted on a radar mast located behind the periscopes. They could be used with the mast above water and the submarine submerged.

Range data from all sources was fed into the TDC. This electromechanical analog computer provided fire control for torpedoes. A sophisticated piece of equipment, it automatically tracked the target based on observations fed into it. The Mk I TDC was introduced in 1938 and retrofitted into all USN submarines. The Mk III, standard through most of World War II, was introduced in 1940 in the Tambor class.

A Mk IV TDC entered service in 1943 and permitted solutions for the Mk 18 electric torpedo.

Getting a torpedo from a USN fleet submarine to a Japanese carrier required precise calculation and a great deal of information. The course and speed of both submarine and target needed to be known accurately and fed into the TDC. By 1942 the observations required came from both periscope sightings and sonar readings. In 1942 radar measurements began to be used and by 1943 they were standard.

To facilitate coordination of these disparate sources of information, the equipment and operators were all crowded into the conning tower along with communications equipment and the submarine's helm. This included the submarine's wheel and main control unit, plan position indicator, radar scope and bearing indicator, the TDC, and the weapons control console. In a very real sense putting this all together created the first Combat Information Center (CIC), even before the concept of the CIC emerged.

Throw in a chart table for navigation, two periscopes (and the working space around them), a radar mast, the radio, and an air-conditioning unit, plus the 10–12 men required to operate all the equipment, and things got crowded. Two hatches, one down to the control room and the rest of the submarine and one up to the bridge, further reduced the space available.

For long-range communications, fleet submarines used radio. Submarines operating in "wolf packs" also communicated using SJ surface search radar. The short range and focused beam provided signal security. World War II submarine radio communication began when the radio mast cleared the surface. Shore-to-submarine communication was done through Fox broadcasts, sent every two hours from COMSUBPAC. Submarines rose to periscope depth at scheduled broadcast times to copy the coded transmission.

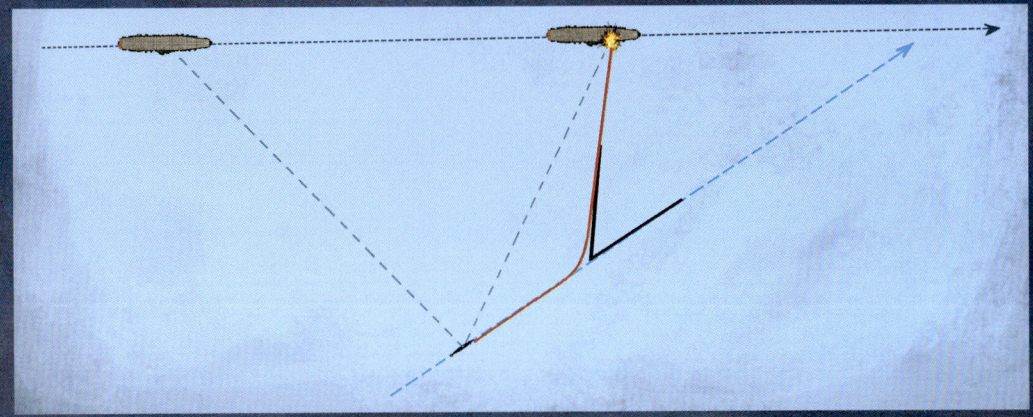

USN TORPEDO DATA COMPUTER

Torpedoes were fitted with a gyroscope that kept a torpedo running straight at a predetermined depth. It turned the torpedo to the final direction after traveling a preset distance from the submarine (known as the "reach"). The "torpedo problem" (an example is shown above) involved determining the gyro angle required to hit the target given a bearing, speed, and range for both the submarine and target.

Different navies used different devices to solve the torpedo problem. The USN used the Torpedo Data Computer (TDC), an electromechanical analog computer that used electrical relays and physical gears for computation. Users entered in bearing, speed, and range information for both the submarine and target and the TDC returned the torpedo gyro angle settings that allowed the torpedo to be aimed at a target without needing to point the submarine in the direction the torpedo needed to travel.

The Mk III TDC, shown in this plate, had two parts: the position keeper (left) and angle solver (right). The position keeper tracked the target and predicted its current position. It automatically provided the submarine's course and speed, while the target's length, course, speed, and angle on the bow were fed in through hand cranks. The angle took position keeper solutions and combined them with the properties of the torpedo to produce a torpedo gyro angle setting.

The plate shows the torpedo problem (top), the assembled TDC (bottom left), and an exploded view showing the TDC's interior (bottom right). While not what we think of today as a computer, the TDC was surprisingly sophisticated for its time.

IJN AIRCRAFT CARRIERS

Imperial Japanese Navy carriers relied largely on their passive defenses and their speed in confrontations with USN fleet submarines. Passive defense included their armor and internal structure. Carriers were singularly ill-prepared to fight duels with submarines, however, and could only engage surfaced submarines. Because the IJN carriers' antiaircraft suite outgunned any fleet submarine, none of the latter that surfaced remained undetected.

The carriers' best means of defense was speed. Most could move faster than a surfaced submarine. Even cruising at 18kn a carrier outran a submerged submarine, and was only marginally slower than a surfaced submarine. This section presents carrier characteristics.

STRUCTURE

The primary protection an aircraft carrier had against submarines was its structure. It had little offensive capability against submarines, relying on its escorts for protection against them. Though a carrier could suffer a tremendous amount of damage above the waterline and survive, a torpedo was dangerous because it could destroy a carrier's underwater integrity. Damage below the waterline reduced a carrier's reserve buoyancy and stability.

A combination of compartmentalization and armor could defeat torpedoes. Both the dreadnoughts converted to aircraft carriers (*Akagi*, *Kaga*, and *Shinano*) and the keel-up carriers designed prewar after expiration of naval treaties (*Shōkaku*, *Zuikaku*, and *Taihō*) had elaborate compartmentalization and heavy armor.

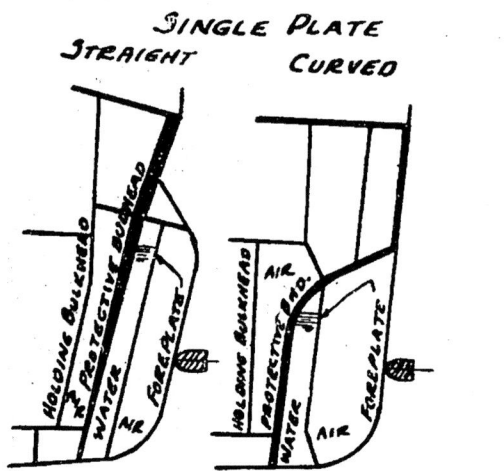
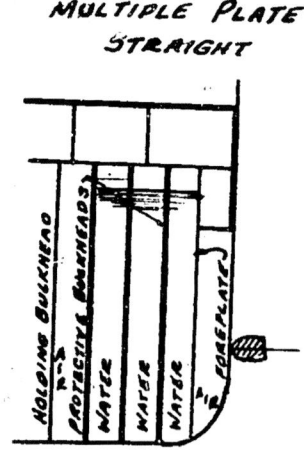

Different internal compartmentalization techniques used to protect Japanese carriers from torpedoes are shown in this drawing. In many cases the armor belt of a carrier was mounted internally, at the protective bulkhead. (AC)

TYPES OF PROTECTION USING WATER LAYERS

IJN TORPEDO PROTECTION

Japanese naval architects incorporated a sophisticated defense in depth to protect aircraft carriers from torpedo hits. This plate illustrates how it worked using a cross-section of a Shōkaku-class carrier. Three layers of compartments shielded the carrier's vitals — the magazines, machinery, and boiler rooms.

The outer layer of compartments was called the double-bottom; an outer and inner layer of plating that followed the profile of the hull. These watertight compartments (WTCs) were used for fuel storage. The bunker fuel used by the boilers was difficult to ignite, and not an explosion hazard. Any torpedo striking the hull would blast a hole in the outer plating, leaving it open to flooding. A small shell or a low-order torpedo explosion would be stopped by the combination of bunker fuel and plating and only the double-bottom would flood.

The middle and inner layers of WTCs were also fuel bunkers. During battle the fuel was drained from the middle layer, while the inner layer was kept full. This allowed the compressible air in the middle compartment to absorb the energy of an explosion too powerful to be contained by the outer WTCs, while the incompressible liquid in the inner WTC reinforced the outer bulkhead of the compartment.

The final layer of defense was the heavily reinforced bulkhead of the boiler room. Often, this was where the belt armor was located if the carrier was armored. (Alternatively, it could cover the exterior bulkhead.) This protected the ship's vitals, even if the inner WTC were compromised.

Theoretically, a Japanese torpedo warhead was powerful enough to compromise all three layers of WTC, while US torpedo warheads were too small to get past the middle layer, as shown in the plate. If a torpedo struck at the intersection of two compartments, it could force the transverse bulkhead back, like a cue stick striking a pool ball, fracturing the longitudinal bulkheads at the junction. This is what happened when the second torpedo struck *Shōkaku*, flooding two boiler rooms.

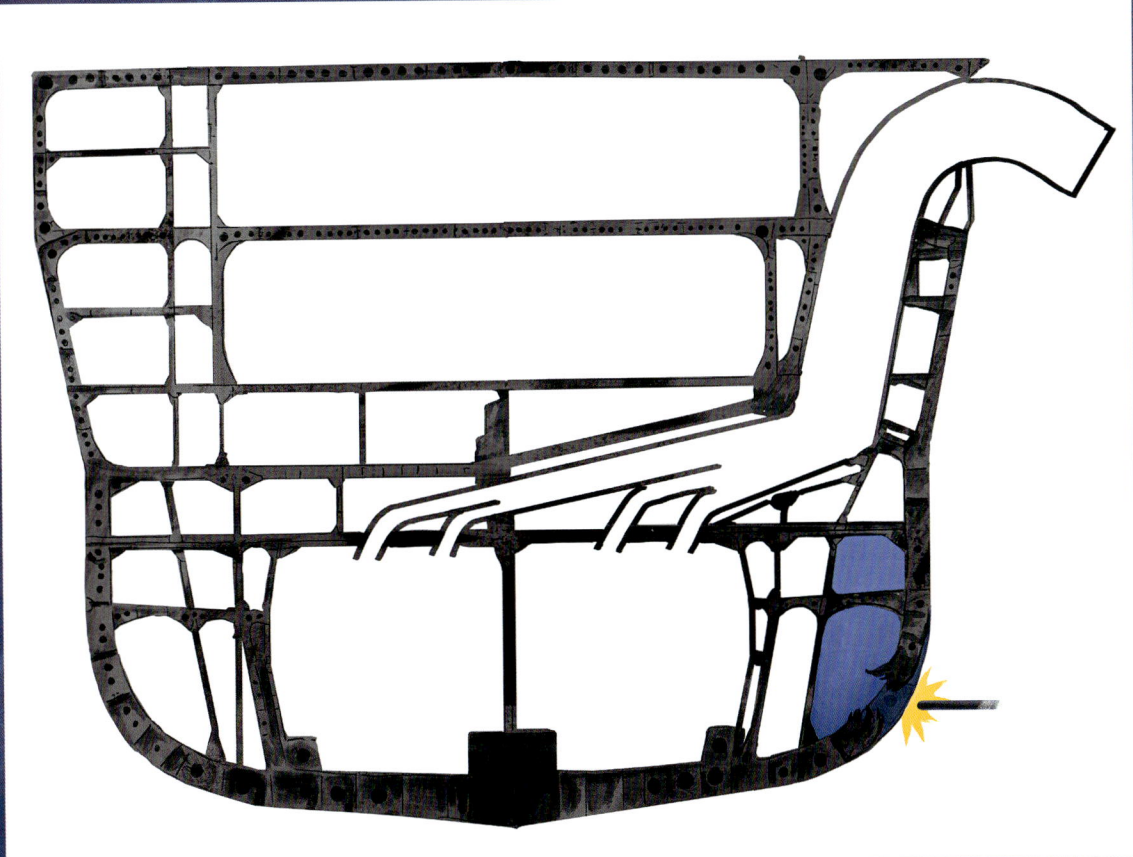

The dreadnoughts retained some of the armor belt planned for their dreadnought role. *Akagi* and *Kaga* had a maximum armor belt thickness of 152mm (6in), with thinner armor on the upper portions of the torpedo bulge and the thickest armor on the lower portions (most likely to be hit by torpedoes). *Shinano* retained the 160–400mm (6.3–15.75in) belt intended for a battleship. *Shōkaku* and *Zuikaku* had a 215mm (8.5in) belt over the machinery spaces, while *Taihō* had a 152mm belt over the machinery. These thicknesses were theoretically sufficient to defeat US torpedoes.

Internally, there were several layers of compartments. The machinery amidships was in a compartment shielded by two or three separate compartments before reaching the side of the ship. While the innermost compartment next to the central compartment housed equipment, the outermost was a void space, often with a second void compartment inside it. A torpedo hitting the side of the ship would blow a hole in the void space, but leave the inner compartments intact. The bulkheads of the central machinery compartment were reinforced to provide a protective vertical bulkhead. Often the belt armor was split into two layers, with one layer on the outside of the ship and the other on the protective vertical bulkhead.

Treaty tonnage limitations undercut using this kind of structural defense on carriers built while the terms of naval treaties were in force. Armor and bulkheads added weight counting against carrier tonnage. Three Japanese carriers built prior to withdrawing from the naval treaties (*Ryūjō*, *Sōryū*, and *Hiryū*) lacked armor and had less compartmentalization. So did the 14 "shadow" carriers, which were converted from fast naval auxiliaries. Many of the wartime conversions added a flight deck and hangar atop a merchant ship's hull, these ships having been built to civilian standards of watertight integrity. Wartime conversions were also hastily done, without much though given to internal structural protection.

Structural protection was effective only when paired with a good damage-control team. This was true for both armored and unarmored carriers. Passive defenses had to be backed up by active defenses. Because compartments flooded by a torpedo hit were on the outside, farthest from the centerline, they threatened a carrier's transverse stability. Unless compartments on the opposite side were counterflooded, the damaged carrier might capsize.

PROPULSION

All Japanese aircraft carriers used steam turbines for propulsion. Two of the "shadow" carriers (*Chitose* and *Chiyoda*), converted from seaplane carriers, used a mix of diesel engines and steam turbines. Japanese carriers depended on speed for operations. Carriers operating offensively had to be capable of making at least 28kn. Carriers incapable of making at least that speed were used as convoy escorts, aircraft carrier/ transports, or training carriers.

The fleet carriers – those capable of carrying 60 or more aircraft – had four shafts and four propellers. Light and escort carriers, along with aircraft carrier/transports, had two shafts and two propellers. There was a limit to the useful power a propeller could accept before hydrodynamics made it ineffective. In World War II this was around 40,000hp per propeller. All two-shaft carriers had an aggregate horsepower below 80,000hp; all four-shaft carriers over 80,000hp.

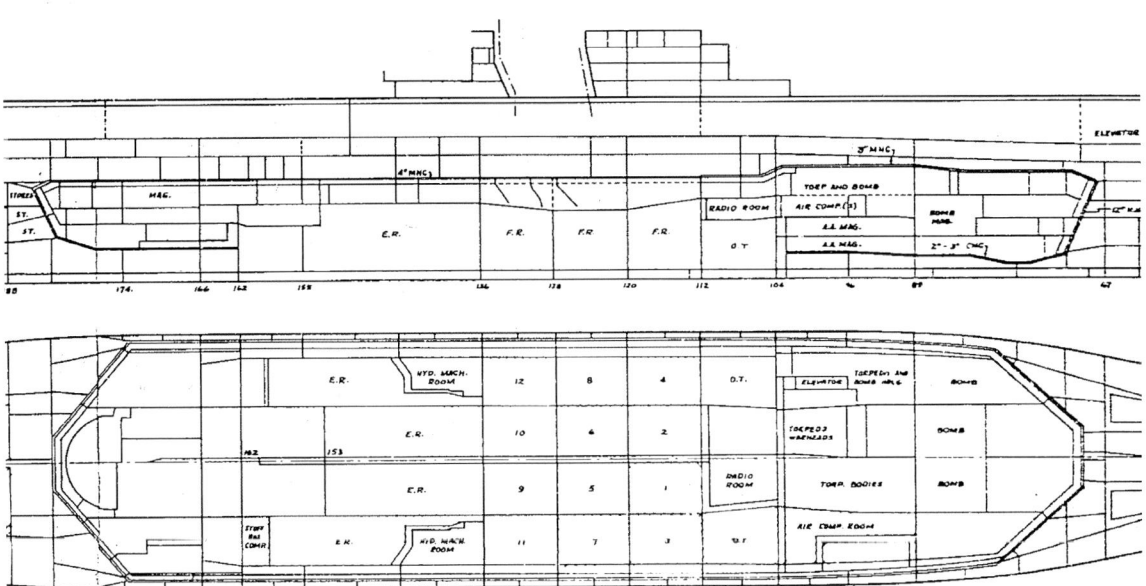

Regardless of the number of shafts, all used Kampon boilers. By World War II these were oil fueled, burning Bunker C oil, a heavy fuel oil. When built, *Akagi* and *Kaga* used a mixture of coal-fired and oil-fired boilers. The coal-fired boilers were replaced with oil-burning boilers during mid-1930s refits. Kampon boilers operated at 427psi, generating a maximum of roughly 18,750shp per boiler. Each boiler consumed 4.67 tons of bunker fuel per hour at maximum operation.

The boilers were connected to geared steam turbines, spun by the steam entering them. There was one turbine per shaft. The speed of the turbines was determined by the volume of steam entering them. To cruise, generally only one boiler was required. Top speed required all boilers at maximum output. Steam could be routed from any boiler to any turbine, thus providing redundancy. Gears reduced the speed of the turbine to the speed required by the propellers. With the diesel–steam hybrids, the diesel engines, with their higher fuel efficiency, were used for cruising with the steam boilers and turbines brought online when high speed was required.

While diesels offered excellent fuel economy they were significantly heavier in terms of horsepower per unit weight than steam plants. Individual diesels produced less power than steam turbines. Because the power required for a given speed increased as the square of the speed, Japan could not cram in enough diesels to push a ship much above 20kn, and so required diesel–steam hybrid arrangements. This required additional and more complicated gearing, because separate gears were used for each power plant.

It also required two fuels be carried: diesel oil for the diesels and bunker oil for the steam plant. While steam boilers could burn diesel oil, it was more expensive than bunker oil. Additionally diesel, while not explosive like gasoline, was more volatile than bunker oil. Bunker C oil had low volatility, being what was left after more volatile elements had been distilled out of crude oil. It could safely be stored in the outside void compartments used for torpedo protection. After the experiment with the Chitoses, Japan stuck to steam plants exclusively.

This drawing illustrates the distribution of machinery in a Japanese carrier. (This is *Shinano*, but the arrangement is typical of large Japanese carriers.) The 12 boilers are in individual watertight rooms (numbered 1–12) amidships. Immediately aft of the boilers are the four engine rooms (E. R.) each containing a steam turbine that drives one of the ship's propellers. (AC)

41

Zuhio as camouflaged at the battle of Leyte Gulf. Through most of the war most Japanese warships were painted in an overall dark gray, including metal decks. Linoleum and wooden decks were left unpainted, except for deck markings on aircraft carriers. Heavy losses in 1942–43 led the Japanese to create a special committee to investigate camouflage patterns for aircraft carriers during March–July 1944. The emphasis was upon reducing carriers' visibility to submarines and confusing USN dive bombers. The committee's work was incomplete when *Taihō* and *Shōkaku* were lost to *Albacore* and *Cavalla* on June 19, 1944, apparently sunk while wearing traditional dark gray. That perhaps spurred adoption of new camouflage measures; a mixture of black and various greens. By October all surviving carriers sported the new camouflage colors, but it did not prevent four (*Zuikaku, Zuihō, Chiyoda*, and *Chitose*) being sunk at the battle of Leyte Gulf on October 23–26. Nor did the dark-green merchant-ship silhouette against a light-green background sported by *Shinano* prevent it from being spotted and sunk by *Archerfish* on November 29, 1944. (AC)

WEAPONRY

Carriers were not equipped with antisubmarine warfare (ASW) weapons such as depth charges or sonar. They typically operated at speeds too great for sonar to work, which made the use of depth charges impractical. Instead, they depended on their escorts to attack submerged submarines. Carriers could, however, use their guns and aircraft to attack surfaced submarines.

While few Japanese carriers mounted the 200mm guns of *Kaga*, all carried 80mm, 120mm, or 127mm heavy antiaircraft guns capable of sinking a submarine. *Kaga*'s 200mm guns are below its funnel, while its 127mm guns are amidships. (Kure City Maritime History and Science Museum/Wikimedia/Public Domain)

Aircraft were among the most effective submarine killers of World War II. Diesel-electric submarines had to surface to recharge their batteries, and patrolling aircraft could spot a submarine well outside a submarine's attack range from a task group or convoy. Aircraft, armed with bombs or depth charges, could attack the submarine. Even if the bombs missed, the attack forced the submarine to submerge, reducing its speed and ability to spot the enemy.

The main armament of an aircraft carrier was its aircraft. Shown here are Mitsubishi A6M Zero fighters, preparing to take off. Japanese carriers rarely carried ASW aircraft, which left them dependent on shore-based ASW aircraft and escorting destroyers to keep submarines from establishing a firing position. (USNHHC)

Although Japanese carrier aircraft could carry depth charges or bombs, early in the war the IJN did not do this, choosing instead to rely on speed to outrun submarines. Even at an 18kn cruising speed a submarine had to be lucky or well-informed to establish a firing position on a carrier group. The IJN also viewed putting carrier aircraft on ASW duties as a waste of an aircraft that could be used to attack enemy ships or bases; and by the time the IJN began fielding ASW aircraft, in the middle of the Pacific War, it was short of carrier-qualified pilots. This meant ASW aircraft were land-based; but even this was enough to make USN submarines wary of daytime surface operations when and where Japan had maritime aircraft.

While Japanese carriers could not attack submerged USN submarines, they had weapons capable of fighting surfaced submarines. All carried guns capable of penetrating a submarine's pressure hull, and generally plenty of them. *Akagi* and *Kaga* both carried ten 200mm (7.9in) guns, five on each side.

These were not the only guns capable of killing a submarine. The carriers' heavy antiaircraft battery could also be used, and IJN carriers carried lots of them. The fleet carriers built prewar had at least 12 127mm (5in) guns by World War II as did the wartime Unryū class and *Shinano. Taihō* had 12 100mm (3.9in) guns. The light carriers had 8–12 127mm guns, as did the Hiyō class. Some of the aircraft carrier/transports and training carriers had lighter batteries with only 76mm (3in) or 120mm (4.7in) guns.

While the primary function of these guns was to protect the carrier from aircraft, and while only half could be brought to bear on a side, they had a high rate of fire. They could easily and swiftly have dispatched a submarine foolish enough to engage in a gunnery duel. The largest deck guns carried by USN fleet submarines were a pair of 6in guns mounted on *V-4* through *V-6*. Most carried single 3in or 5in guns.

ELECTRONICS

During World War II, Japan's electronics development lagged behind that of all major powers, Allied and Axis, except perhaps that of Italy. Japan had competent design engineers; what was lacking was interest in pushing development of radio and radar systems. Additionally, Japan's industrial base was inadequate for mass production of electronic components.

Japanese naval radar development began in April 1941 with the Type 2 Mk 1 shore-based search radar. Work on a ship-based system, the Type 21, began in October 1941. An operational version was released in August 1943. It had a mattress antenna, operated at the 1.5m wavelength, and had a range of 70–100km (38–54NM) with an accuracy of 1–2km (0.54–1.08NM). It was used for both air and surface search, and could pick out a formation of aircraft or a large surface ship, but was unlikely to detect a submarine hull awash with just the conning tower above water. It would almost certainly not pick up a radar mast.

These ship-based systems began to be installed on IJN aircraft carriers and battleships in the fourth quarter of 1942, prior to which IJN ships lacked radar. The Type 13 was supplemented by the Type 3 in February 1944 or the Type 22 in December 1943. The Type 13 was a 2m-wavelength radar with a 50–100km (27–54NM) range. Using Yagi antennae, it was less accurate than the Type 21, but was one-eighth its weight. The Type 22 was a microwave surface search radar with a horn antenna. While more accurate than earlier radars, it was also less reliable.

The IJN lagged behind in radar development, although by 1943 most of its carriers had radar. The Yagi antennae of *Jun'yō's* Type 13 radar can be seen here on the carrier's after mast. Its Type 21 "mattress" is visible at the front of the island. (USNHHC)

Japan also developed radio and radar detection finders. These could detect the direction of either a radio or radar broadcast, but they were accurate to only +5 degrees. This gave the general direction of the broadcasting radio or radar, but was not accurate enough for targeting purposes, which depended on detecting a signal.

Submarine radio and SD radar transmissions, which were omnidirectional, were more likely to be detected than the focused SJ radar. SJ radar would only be picked up when the radar was pointed directly at the ship equipped with the detector; but the detector only gave bearing, not range. The detector's primary function was to warn the ship carrying it that they were under radar observation.

USN submarine commanders constantly worried about Japanese radar and radar detectors; but Japanese electronics were simply not good enough to pose a threat to an alert submarine skipper. Japanese radar would almost certainly not pick up a submarine's radar mast; and a carrier's radar detectors were unlikely to capture SJ transmissions if the submarine used intermittent observations.

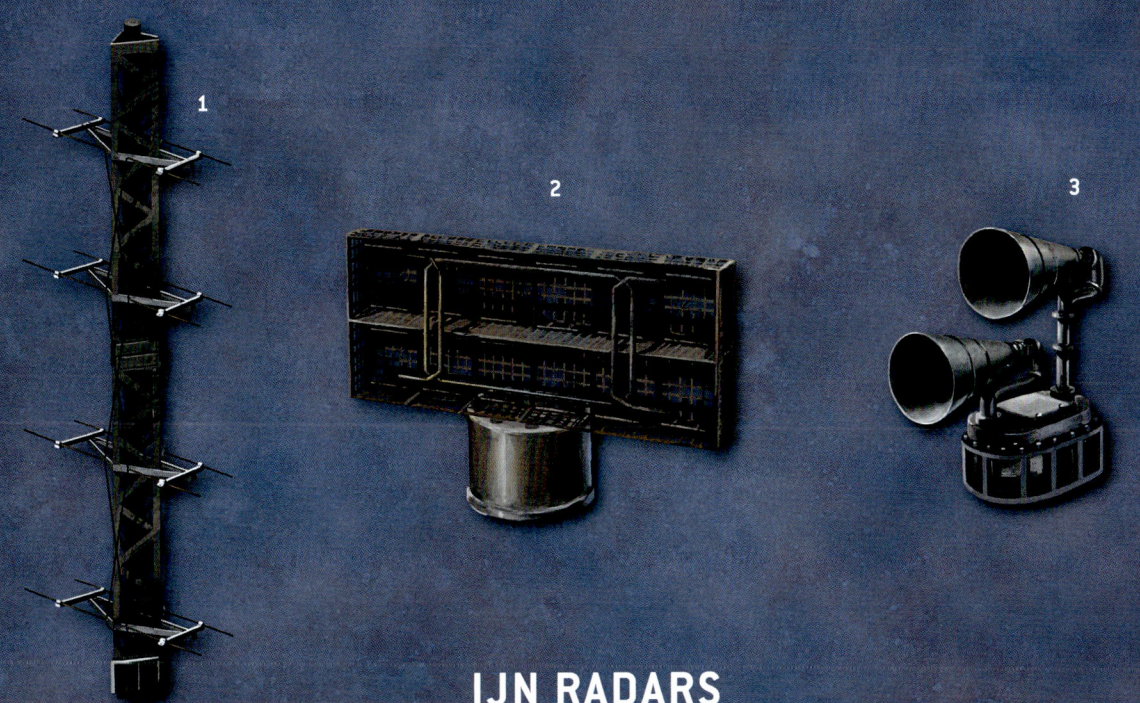

IJN RADARS

While the IJN employed many different radar systems during World War II, during the period covered by this book, its warships mounted the Type 13 air search (**1**), the Type 21 surface search (**2**), and Type 22 general-purpose (**3**) radars (not shown to scale). Their performance is given in the table below.

IJN radar performance			
	Type 13	**Type 21**	**Type 22**
Wavelength (cm)	200	150	10
Pulse width (microseconds)	10	10	10
Pulse repetition frequency (Hz)	500	1,000	2,500
Power (kW)	10	5	2
Range (NM)	30–60 (aircraft)	60 (aircraft group); 40 (single aircraft); 12 (large ship)	20 (aircraft group); 10 (single aircraft); 13 (large ship)
Antenna	Vertical dipole transmitter; Yagi receiver	Mattress: two horizontal sets of four dipoles (transmitter) and two horizontal sets of three dipoles (receiver)	Horn
Accuracy	Unknown	~1NM	220yd
Resolution	N/A	2,200yd/20 degrees	1,600yd/40 degrees
Weight on ship (lb)	240	1,850	2,910

Japanese radar development lagged behind that of the United States by at least a year and fewer IJN warships were equipped with radar. Its performance was inferior to USN radars commonly used on fleet submarines. While *Sailfish* could accurately launch torpedoes at *Chūyō* using only radar observations, *Chūyō*'s Type 21 radar lacked the resolution to detect *Sailfish*'s radar mast or periscope under typhoon conditions. The Type 22 centimeter-wave radar could have done so, but it only began to see widespread operational use in late 1944, too late for Japan's carriers.

THE COMBATANTS

Battles between USN submarines and IJN aircraft carriers pitted two disparate sets of warriors against each other. The submariner was part of an elite, highly trained, and picked group of men. Submarines had small crews, operating independently. Without the best men, failure was assured. The sailors and officers who served aboard USN submarines in World War II were elite volunteers among volunteers.

The Japanese sailor aboard an aircraft carrier was typically a conscript. Carriers were the most important warships Japan possessed and had large crews, but they had to make do with the manpower left over after naval services with more rigorous standards got first pick of the available recruits. Under normal circumstances this worked well enough because carriers were part of a larger force, and could rely on external resources for support.

While the two groups of men differed, they also shared common traits. Both were patriotic, willing to fight and, if necessary, die for their country. Both were motivated to do their best, whether volunteer submariners or conscript carrier sailors. Both came from countries with long and victorious maritime traditions, and drew pride from that. Both were used to winning and expected to win.

USN SUBMARINERS

The submarine service was small. Fewer than 18,000 submariners served in it during the war – only 2 percent of the USN's manpower – of whom 3,506 died during hostilities. A total of 52 submarines were lost. Yet the submarine service contributed materially to the United States' victory in the Pacific War. Submariners correctly viewed themselves as an elite service. Up until January 1943 every man who joined the USN was a volunteer; and to serve aboard a submarine a sailor had to volunteer for submarine duty and go through and pass a rigorous submarine school. Even after qualification, service remained voluntary. A submariner could request transfer from submarine duty whenever he was on shore.

During the 1920s and 1930s the USN relied on highly professional long-service sailors in both enlisted and officer ranks. During the Depression years of the 1930s, when civilian jobs were scarce, the USN was highly selective of those permitted to serve, allowing only the best to re-enlist. This changed with the start of World War II on September 1, 1939.

Although the United States was neutral through December 7, 1941, it anticipated entry to the war and so began preparations to expand the USN in the late 1930s, including vastly expanded numbers of both enlisted and commissioned personnel. The prewar officers and men served as a cadre for the wartime USN with its reserve officers and wartime enlistees. Despite rapid expansion, however, enlistment in the USN remained voluntary through the first year of the war. The growth of the USN was such that on February 1, 1943, it ended voluntary enlistment of men aged between 18 and 37 inclusive, turning to conscription to fill its ranks. Even with the boost to numbers conscription brought, 60 percent of those who served in the USN during World War II, including all officers, were volunteers.

The USN had higher physical and mental standards for enlistment than the US Army prior to and through January 1943. The higher standards were needed as the USN was a highly technical service in the mid-20th century. Many preferred USN service due to better living conditions and the opportunity to learn skills transferrable to peacetime employment. Conscription was run by the Selective Service System, however, which procured men for both the USN and US Army. Thereafter, US Army standards were used for recruits of both services.

Training began when an individual entered the USN, and ended when he left it. All men enlisting in the USN began their careers at Navy Boot Camp. Prior to World War II there were four boot camps (San Diego, California; Bainbridge, Maryland; Newport, Rhode Island; and Great Lakes, Illinois). During World War II three more were added (Norfolk, Virginia; Sampson, New York; and Farragut, Idaho). Boot Camp normally lasted six weeks.

During World War II, depending on the needs of the USN for personnel, Boot Camp could be shortened to as little as four weeks or lengthened to eight weeks. At Boot Camp, recruits were issued their uniform and kit (including a copy of *The Bluejacket's Manual*) and learned the fundamentals of being a sailor: basic drill,

Sailors volunteered for submarine service, but to serve aboard a submarine, whether commissioned or enlisted, they had to pass submarine school. This combined rigorous classroom training with practical exercises aboard training submarines. (USNHHC)

seamanship, naval customs and courtesy, small-arms training, swimming, and how to live aboard ship.

Upon graduation, the new seamen were either assigned directly to ships, on which they learned their duties through what was essentially an apprenticeship, or were assigned to one of three categories of school (Class A to Class C) where they received specialty training.

Class A schools provided elementary instruction to recruits in technical fields and gave them the groundwork necessary to move into the lowest petty-officer ratings. The instruction included a broad range of specialties: electrical, ordnance, communications, clerical, machinists, metalworkers, woodworkers, radiomen, diesel-engine mechanics, hospital corpsmen, even bugling.

Class B schools gave enlisted men more advanced instruction in more complex machinery such as bombsights, optics, or gyro compasses, firefighting, or torpedoman training. Typically men attending these schools already had some experience in the USN, and so were not raw recruits.

Class C schools were more advanced still, providing training for subjects not normally a part of shipboard instruction. Men accepted into these schools were either in the top part of their recruit class for Class A schools or had demonstrated superior capability during sea service.

To join the submarine service, candidates volunteered; something they could do at any stage after completing boot training. Volunteers were evaluated for their fitness, going through a one-week evaluation period. Physical, mental, and psychological factors were assessed. This included overall physical fitness, night vision, and susceptibility to claustrophobia or stress. They also had to successfully perform simulated submarine escapes in a 100ft water-filled tower. Candidates who passed this screening process were admitted to the submarine school. Only 10 percent of those going through this evaluation survived elimination, however. The rest were returned to other duties.

Once admitted to submarine school, they went through weeks of training. The first few weeks were split between training classes and practical exercises. It was like a return to boot camp. Trainees maintained workbooks covering the systems they learned. On Monday of each week they were tested on the previous week's material,

HERMAN J. KOSSLER

Herman Joseph Kossler was born on December 8, 1911, in Portsmouth, Virginia, where he grew up. His parents were Herman J. Kossler and Octavie A. Kossler (née Barraud). Kossler obtained an appointment to the US Naval Academy at Annapolis, Maryland, while in his late teens, graduating in the Annapolis Class of 1934.

Kossler became a career naval officer, following a typical promotion path in the prewar peacetime USN (ensign upon graduation and commissioning, lieutenant junior grade in 1937, lieutenant in 1941). He joined the submarine service prior to the United States' entry into World War II. By May 1942 he was executive officer of *Guardfish*, a newly launched Gato-class boat.

Guardfish's skipper was one of the USN's outstanding captains, Thomas B. Klaking, US Naval Academy Class of 1927. Klaking and Kossler proved to be an excellent command team. In the four war patrols Kossler served under Klaking, *Guardfish* sank ten Japanese ships totaling 33,122 tons (as credited by the postwar Joint Army–Navy Assessment Committee). This included a legendary first war patrol on which *Guardfish* penetrated Tokyo Bay and sank five ships. (In a post-patrol press conference Klaking claimed to have gotten so close to shore that they watched horse races. It was a "sea story," but Kossler did not contradict it at the time. The story raised morale stateside.)

Kossler was promoted to lieutenant commander in March 1943, during his stint in *Guardfish*. The following year, on February 1, 1944, he was promoted to commander. By then he was captain of *Cavalla*, that submarine's first. He would remain as skipper of *Cavalla* until January 18, 1946, its only World War II commander.

During six war patrols under Kossler, *Cavalla* sank four ships for 34,580 tons. Besides *Shōkaku*, Kossler's bag included the Akizuki-class destroyer *Shimotsuki* (2,700 tons) and the net tenders *Kankō Maru* (909GRT) and *Shunsen Maru* (909GRT). The relatively low score was due to a general scarcity of targets after July 1944 and *Cavalla* being used for reconnaissance, lifeguard, and escort duties on three of its patrols.

Kossler and *Cavalla* were off the coast of Japan when Japan surrendered on August 15, 1945, entered Tokyo Bay with Allied warships on August 31, and were present at the

Herman J. Kossler, as a USN commander during the Korean War. (USNHHC)

surrender ceremonies on September 2. On October 6, *Cavalla* sailed to New London from Tokyo Bay, where Kossler relinquished command on January 18, 1946.

Kossler remained in the USN after World War II, serving during the Korean and Vietnam wars, eventually attaining the rank of rear admiral. Owing to a lack of senior submarine commands, Kossler left submarines. In 1960, as a captain he commanded Amphibious Squadron 10. As a rear admiral he commanded the Sixth Naval District (which encompassed Georgia and South and North Carolina) during July 1968–November 1973. It was headquartered in Charleston, South Carolina.

Kossler retired from the USN in 1973, settling in Charleston, where he died on July 1, 1988, at age 76. He is buried, along with his second wife, Ursula B. Breher (née Small), at the Beaufort National Cemetery in Beaufort, South Carolina.

needing a score of 70 to pass. If they failed, they could retake a test, but were eliminated if they failed a test twice.

Those who remained began training on actual submarines in the fourth week, aboard obsolete O- and R-class boats. Over the next few weeks trainees went from going through a first dive to operating all the systems aboard a submarine. Those who successfully completed training graduated, and were assigned to working submarines after a two-week leave. Even then their training was not complete. They had to qualify as submariners aboard their new submarine by demonstrating proficiency during their tour.

Most submariners were white; all were male. African Americans and Asians (Chinese and Filipinos) could only serve as messmen or stewards. Hispanics and Native Americans were treated as "White" for service purposes.

Prior to World War II the USN's officer corps was largely made up of long-serving, professional officers. Most were graduates of the United States Naval Academy at Annapolis, Maryland. These men had gone through a four-year training period, including a college education and summer cruises. Officers were expected to be gentlemen as well as mariners. In the USN that meant they were expected to have a college education, and serve as leaders.

With the expansion of the fleet, which began in 1935, the USN realized this corps was too small for the intended growth. To increase numbers it initiated a Naval Reserve Officer Training Corps (ROTC) school system at colleges and universities, where students received naval training along with their baccalaureate degrees, gaining a reserve commission upon graduation. This included men attending maritime academies receiving training to serve as merchant marine officers.

During World War II, ROTC training was vastly expanded, including the creation of the V-7 program in June 1940 and the V-12 program in July 1943. V-7 candidates attended college and went through an eight-month United States Naval Reserve Midshipmen's School, receiving an ensign's commission upon graduation. V-12 midshipmen attended civilian colleges, supplementing that education with roughly 12 months' training to become a naval officer.

The V-7 program was intended to create 36,000 officers, while the V-12 had a target of 200,000 officers. By the time World War II ended, these programs had created 97,000 officers. Another 131,000 were appointed directly from civilian life, including many with prewar college degrees who went through Reserve Officer training. (In some cases these men received rapid promotion based on their existing experience and skills.)

The men who served aboard USN submarines were generally younger and more athletic than those assigned to larger warships. Submarines were cramped and living conditions difficult; and they operated autonomously, in enemy-held waters on patrols that lasted a month or potentially longer. Crews had to be competent and self-reliant to survive. Officers had to be both aggressive and realistic to succeed.

In the early years of the Pacific War submarine crews were largely made up of long-service regulars, both officers and men. Initially, most officers and all commanders were Naval Academy graduates. While reserve officers began serving aboard submarines in 1942, it was not until 1944 that reservists began to command submarines. Similarly, senior enlisted leadership positions were exclusively held by prewar regulars during the war's early years and continued to be dominated by them throughout the war.

IJN PERSONNEL

Established in 1868, the IJN trained hard and fought hard. By the late 1880s it had established a tradition that stressed the importance of training, and the promotion of officers and men based on competence and leadership ability. Hard training and the demand for excellent performance from its personnel led the IJN to victory in the Russo-Japanese War (1904–05). The IJN was seen as a key player thereafter.

Life aboard Japanese warships was spartan. There were few amenities, and training was hard and continual. The IJN, like all Japan's military forces, emphasized offensive capabilities to the exclusion of all else. "Luxuries" such as air conditioning, comfortable quarters, and elaborate rations were seen as consuming resources and space that could be better used to improve combat capability.

Sea duty was emphasized, as were ships' offensive capabilities. The IJN had a series of shore establishments to teach technical skills associated with a warship, including engineering, gunnery, and torpedo schools. The final polish on these skills was to be gained at sea, however, aboard ship during exercises.

Prewar Japan carried out battle training under conditions as close to battle as possible. Maneuvers were conducted in waters distant from Japan where they could be practiced unobserved. The stormy North Pacific was a particularly favored location. Training cruises under combat conditions continued for a month with no weekends, no rest and little sleep during training operations. One drill followed another, and included frequent live-fire exercises. Casualties among personnel were accepted as the price that had to be paid for readiness.

In its formative years the IJN modeled itself on Britain's Royal Navy. As with the Royal Navy, the IJN typically avoided peacetime conscription and kept it to a minimum during wartime. Prior to 1937 there were relatively few conscripts because most manpower needs were filled by volunteers. These volunteers typically came from Hokkaido or Northern Honshu, areas with short growing seasons and low fertility. Young Japanese men viewed the IJN as a means of obtaining technical skills, thereby offering a way out of life on small farms and the poverty of rural life.

After Japan withdrew from the 1922 Washington and 1930 London naval limitations treaties the IJN grew substantially. Between 1928 and 1935 it expanded from 80,595 officers and men to 97,986; a 21.6 percent growth over seven years, with an annual average growth of 2.2 percent. This rate of expansion was manageable. Between 1936 and 1941, however, the IJN grew from 107,547 to 311,359 officers and men, a near 300 percent increase. A further 110,000 personnel were added by the end of 1942.

The expansion of the IJN forced it to rely increasingly on conscription. By the start of the Pacific War only 30 percent of Japan's ratings and noncommissioned officers were volunteers; 70 percent were conscripted. After 1942 conscription declined to 50 percent as men volunteered for the IJN in preference to being drafted into the IJA. Conscription filled the ranks, but not necessarily with the men the IJN most desired. Especially after the start of the Second Sino-Japanese War (1937–45) the IJA, which administered all conscription, ensured its own needs were met before sending men to the IJN. These conscripts were inferior to men received earlier.

An IJN sailor. Life in the IJN was spartan. Sailors lived in plain barracks ashore and crowded conditions aboard ship. Food was plain, but adequate. (AC)

These two Japanese sailors display IJN insignia. The IJN offered opportunities for advancement to those who joined. It provided technical training that would be useful after discharge and gave competent enlistees the chance to progress to petty- and warrant-officer positions. (AC)

Sailors to crew Japan's warships were drawn from Japan's farmers, laborers, and factory workers. All men were subject to conscription at age 20. If conscripted into the IJN, men served three years before discharge. Men could also volunteer to serve a five-year term if they were aged between 17 and 21. Sailors had to demonstrate literacy and competence in basic mathematics and pass a physical examination before being accepted.

Conscripts and volunteers alike could continue in the IJN at the end of their terms. Many did, often remaining in service until retirement age. They could become petty officers and warrant officers, but sailors, regardless of rank, were ineligible for officer commissions. Unlike the USN, Japanese petty and warrant officers did not supervise watches. Sailors were pensioned off at age 40. Petty officers could remain until age 45, with warrant and senior warrant officers retiring at age 50 and 55, respectively.

All IJN officers were volunteers. Entry started at the Imperial Japanese Naval Academy at Etajima. Applications to become line officers were made between the ages of 16 and 19. By the 1930s family status helped, but only in that someone from a Navy family or otherwise well-connected was likely to be better prepared than an outsider. Regardless of their family, applicants had to pass a physical examination and competitive academic examination. Only the top 15 percent of applicants were accepted to the academy.

Line-officer cadets attended three years of classes with a final year aboard a training ship. Engineering cadets spent four years including a year at the Yokosuka engineering academy. All cadets had to pass an examination to receive a commission. If they failed, they retook the examination six months later, but were eliminated if they failed again.

Officers were typically promoted from *kaigun-shōi* (ensign, the lowest commissioned rank) to *kaigun-shōsa* (lieutenant commander) after eight years' service. Subsequent promotion was based on performance through board reviews. Officers experienced "up-or-out" promotions. A lieutenant retired at age 42 if not promoted.

The IJN's expansion created a shortage of officers. Prior to the prewar buildup, admission to the officer corps assumed everyone receiving a commission and demonstrating competence would retire as a captain. Academy class sizes were kept small through the 1920s and early 1930s. Even after the expansion of the IJN began, increased class sizes were based on the number of officers needed as and when new ships were completed, without making allowances for the numbers of officers that would be needed in ten years, after the buildup was completed. As a consequence of this short-sighted calculation, by 1941 there was a shortage of over 1,100 officers.

The shortage of officers could not be filled by Japan's miniscule reserve officer program, because most reserve officers were graduates of the Maritime Academy and Merchant Marine School. These men were needed to run Japan's merchant fleet, even after the war started. The shortage was particularly acute for mid-level officers; the lieutenant commanders and commanders. Wartime casualties aggravated the problem.

ABE TOSHIO

Abe Toshio was born on April 27, 1896, in Ehime, a prefecture in the northwest quarter of Shikoku Island, then largely rural. He attended the Imperial Japanese Naval Academy at Etajima during World War I as part of the Etajima Class 46. On November 21, 1918, he graduated 50th in a class of 124 as a midshipman.

After ten months aboard the armored cruiser *Tokiwa*, he was promoted to sub-lieutenant on August 1, 1919. While in that rank he was a junior officer aboard a cruiser and pre-dreadnought battleship before attending basic torpedo and gunnery courses. Promoted to junior lieutenant in December 1921, he spent a year aboard the battleship *Nagato*, three months on a destroyer, and 14 months as an officer on the armored cruiser *Yakumo*. After two months ashore at the Yokosuka naval district, he was promoted to lieutenant on December 1, 1924. He spent a year taking the Torpedo School Advanced Course.

Abe spent the next four years as a torpedo specialist, serving as torpedo officer aboard two different destroyers and the light cruiser *Nagara*, and as an instructor at the torpedo and naval engineer schools. He was promoted to lieutenant commander while an instructor at the Torpedo School on December 1, 1930. A year later, on December 1, 1931, he became captain of the destroyer *Fumizuki*. Later he commanded the river gunboat *Fushimi* on the Yangtze River.

In March 1935 Abe returned to the Torpedo School as an instructor. He was promoted to commander on November 15, 1935, and continued as an instructor at various technical schools through August 1937. On August 16, 1937, he was made chief equipping officer for the destroyer *Yamagumo*, responsible for outfitting and commissioning the just-launched ship. Four months later, he took command of the destroyer *Asagiri*.

After a year commanding *Asagiri*, on December 15, 1938, Abe was assigned to shore duty as a member of the staff of the 1st Auxiliary Base Unit. He took command of the 21st Destroyer Division on November 15, 1939, and was promoted to captain exactly a year later. During September 1941–March 1942 he commanded the 8th Destroyer Division and during March 1942–January 1943 the 10th Destroyer Division.

While commanding the 10th Destroyer Division Abe distinguished himself during the battle of Midway (June 4–7, 1942), using his flagship, the destroyer *Kazagumo*, to fight fires aboard the carrier *Hiryū* after it had been hit by bombs. He boarded *Hiryū* in an unsuccessful attempt to convince Rear Admiral Yamaguchi Tamon and Captain Kaku Tomeo not to go down with the ship.

In February 1943 Abe was made head of the Torpedo School and chief of the bureau of research there. After over two years in post, he returned to a seagoing assignment as captain of the light cruiser *Ōyodo* in May 1944. On August 15 he was reassigned, becoming the chief equipping officer for the carrier *Shinano*, at that time being built at Yokosuka Naval Arsenal, supervising its construction, launch, and outfitting. On October 1, four days before *Shinano*'s launch and despite a lack of carrier experience, he was named captain of the carrier.

Owing to fears of USAAF B-29 Superfortress long-range bombing raids, and concerns about the quality of construction work at Yokosuka Naval Arsenal, Abe was ordered to complete the outfitting of *Shinano* at Kure Naval Arsenal. The incomplete carrier sailed on November 28, 1944, despite his request to postpone sailing. After *Shinano* was torpedoed on November 29, he opted to continue on to Kure. The carrier began listing, however, and eventually capsized. Despite his 1942 advice to Yamaguchi and Kaku to the contrary, Abe chose to go down with *Shinano*. He was posthumously promoted to rear admiral.

Abe Toshio as a captain. (Toshihide A/Wikimedia/CC BY-SA 4.0)

Junior officers were easily found by accelerating training, but officers with the necessary experience to fill mid-level positions aboard large ships or command of destroyers and smaller vessels became increasingly hard to find.

By 1943 inexperienced and unqualified officers were being pushed into those positions, though doing so probably affected the warships less than it did other parts of the IJN. Less effective officers and men were shuffled off to fleet auxiliaries and shore postings, which reduced overall fleet readiness, but was consistent with the Japanese view prioritizing warriors over artisans and administrators.

Even then there were not enough first-rate candidates to fill all warship slots, so choices still had to be made. The very best officers and men were put into the most challenging positions. They were assigned to destroyers, as naval aviators, and positions aboard major warships associated directly with combat. They manned the guns, operated the torpedoes, and ran the engines. Aboard carriers this included the air division, especially the men who armed and serviced aircraft.

The mediocre had to go somewhere, however. Some were sent to ASW ships, *Kaibōkan*, and patrol craft. ASW held a low priority in the IJN, yet the large warships – cruisers, battleships, and carriers – created the biggest demand for seagoing personnel. The inept, inexperienced, indifferent, and mediocre filled out numbers on these ships. They ended up filling roles necessary to a warship, but secondary to its fighting ability: storekeepers, cooks, and laundrymen. They also performed duties associated with damage control. It was not that the IJN viewed damage control as unimportant – it was and these men were kept busy – but it was not *as* important as guns, torpedoes, and aircraft; hardware that struck the enemy. Damage control was reactive. The result was that the IJN's lesser lights found themselves left in charge of damage control in some of their most important warships – their carriers.

Crewmen work on the forecastle of *Hōshō*. Owing to the vast numbers of men required to man the IJN's carriers, many of those assigned to these ships were not the best available. (USNHHC)

COMBAT

Between 1942 and 1945 there were over 60 encounters in which USN fleet submarines fought IJN carriers during the Pacific War. The five battles described here illustrate the major outcomes that resulted when the two combatants fought one another.

The encounter between *Nautilus* and *Kaga* illustrates what most commonly happened: failure to damage the carrier by the submarine, despite bold efforts. The battle between *Sailfish* and *Chūyō* describes a duel virtually unique in the Pacific War, one in which the submarine made multiple attacks to sink its quarry.

The battles between *Albacore* and *Taihō* and *Cavalla* and *Shōkaku* took place hours apart, yet were very different in nature. With *Taihō*, although only one torpedo fired by *Albacore* hit, it should not have been fatal. The fact that it proved to be so was due to poor Japanese ship design and damage control. By contrast, *Shōkaku* took multiple hits from *Cavalla* that inflicted too much damage to contain.

The final battle examined in this study, between *Archerfish* and *Shinano*, showed how fortune favors the bold. Lieutenant Commander Joseph F. Enright, commanding *Archerfish*, conducted a tricky attack that resulted in multiple torpedo hits; but even this was not enough to sink the massive IJN aircraft carrier. Rather, it was structural weaknesses unrecognized by its commander, Captain Abe Toshio, that caused *Shinano* to sink.

NAUTILUS VS *KAGA*, JUNE 4, 1942

Prior to the battle of Midway, COMSUBPAC assigned no fewer than 11 fleet submarines in two arcs around Midway Atoll to intercept the incoming Japanese forces. When US aircraft operating from the atoll made contact with the Japanese, three USN boats (*Gudgeon*, *Grouper*, and *Nautilus*) were in position to intercept the IJN's *Kidō Butai* (Mobile Force aka First Air Fleet): four fleet carriers, two battleships, three cruisers, and 11 destroyers. *Gudgeon* and *Grouper* were quickly forced down by IJN destroyers and aircraft. Once the boats were deep, their unaggressive skippers kept them deep, playing no further part in the battle.

Nautilus was commanded by Lieutenant Commander William H. Brockman, a man with a different temperament. His boat picked up the contact report from US aircraft at 0544hrs. Concluding that the *Kidō Butai* could cross the northern boundary of his patrol area, he moved to intercept, submerged. At 0555hrs he was rewarded with the sight of masts spotted by *Nautilus*'s periscope. Strafed by a circling Japanese aircraft, he lowered the periscope and continued course.

At 0800hrs Brockman raised the periscope again and saw four IJN warships. The battleship *Kirishima* and the cruiser *Nagara* were in column with two destroyers off either side ahead of the larger ships. As he set an attack on *Kirishima*, the nearest destroyer turned and charged *Nautilus*. Brockman took *Nautilus* deep, unable to fire. The destroyer rumbled overhead, dropping 20 depth charges, but all were set too shallow to hurt the boat.

Brockman stayed deep for 24 minutes before returning to periscope depth. IJN ships were all around, 3,000yd distant. This included *Kirishima*, which opened up with its main guns, firing at the periscope. Brockman ordered two torpedoes fired: one failed to launch; the other missed the battleship.

The destroyer came in again, sonar pinging. Brockman took *Nautilus* down to 150ft with depth charges bursting around the boat. No damage was done. Eventually the destroyer broke off, returning to the *Kidō Butai*. Brockman returned to periscope depth. This time he spotted a carrier moving closer at high speed. Before he could set up an attack, however, the destroyer charged once again. Annoyed and hoping to

Nautilus off Mare Island, California, in April 1942, following a refit. This shows the boat as it would have appeared at the battle of Midway. With its high freeboard and 6in deck guns, *Nautilus* was one of the most distinctive USN boats. (USNHHC)

discourage it, Brockman fired one torpedo at the destroyer. It dodged, the torpedo missed, and the destroyer charged *Nautilus*. Once again Brockman took his boat deep. The destroyer dropped eight depth charges where it thought *Nautilus* was.

Nautilus stayed deep, creeping in the direction it had seen the carrier moving until the destroyer finally gave up and went away. *Nautilus* surfaced around 1000hrs. The ocean was empty. Thirty minutes later pillars of smoke were seen on the horizon, 11NM distant. Five minutes earlier, USN dive bombers from the carriers *Enterprise* and *Yorktown* had found the *Kidō Butai*, and hit the carriers *Sōryū*, *Akagi*, and *Kaga*. *Nautilus* picked up the dive bombers' radio report that a Japanese carrier was hit. *Nautilus* moved toward the smoke.

At 1145hrs Brockman saw the smoke was rising from a motionless and burning carrier 8NM away. *Nautilus* continued toward it, submerged. As they neared, Brockman and his executive officer Lieutenant Roy S. Benson took turns to view the stricken carrier through the periscope in an attempt to identify it. They finally decided it was *Sōryū*. The carrier's crew, preoccupied with damage control, allowed *Nautilus* to close undetected. At 2,700yd Brockman decided to attack. Four torpedoes were readied.

Spacing the shots 90 seconds apart, *Nautilus* began launching the torpedoes at 1359hrs. One failed to launch; the other three sped toward the carrier. Brockman watched as fresh explosions rocked the carrier. There were five USN officers in the boat's conning tower, all of whom took turns looking through the periscope. Then destroyers attacked *Nautilus*, and Brockman took the boat down to 300ft, convinced

57

he had just sunk an IJN carrier. He had not actually seen it sink, however, and stated as much in his patrol report.

Brockman's efforts were betrayed by faulty torpedoes, two of which missed the carrier altogether. The third struck amidships, but did not explode. The issue was most probably the torpedo's firing pin, which – unknown at the time – was too weak. Tests a year later revealed that a perfect shot – a hit perpendicular to the target – crushed the torpedo's exploder mechanism before it detonated the warhead.

Brockman's shot was perfect; but the carrier hit was *Kaga*, not *Sōryū*. The third torpedo smashed into *Kaga*'s 152mm armor belt and shattered. The air flask of the dud torpedo popped free, floated to the surface, and served as an unexpected floatation device for *Kaga* crewmen already in the water. It was poor payment for a determined effort by Brockman and the crew of *Nautilus*.

Brockman was rewarded when he returned to Pearl Harbor, credited with sinking a 10,000-ton carrier. He received a Navy Cross for his efforts and remained in command of *Nautilus* for five war patrols through May 1943, earning two more Navy Crosses, and later commanded *Halibut*. Postwar he was credited with sinking six ships – but no carriers. Lieutenant Benson, promoted to lieutenant commander and then commander, went on to captain *Trigger* and *Razorback*, sinking five ships.

SAILFISH VS *CHŪYŌ*, DECEMBER 4, 1943

On November 30, 1943, the light carrier *Zuihō* and escort carriers *Un'yō* and *Chūyō* departed the Japanese base at Truk in the Caroline Islands. *Zuihō* was one of Japan's "shadow" carriers, originally built as a submarine tender. *Un'yō* and *Chūyō* were two of three 22kn, 17,100GRT fast passenger liners converted to escort carriers. The three carriers were shuttling aircraft from Japan to Truk. US codebreakers detected their departure and alerted *Skate*, *Gunnel*, and *Sailfish*. Unknown to Naval Intelligence,

Un'yō and *Chūyō* were also carrying POWs from *Sculpin*, scuttled off Truk on November 19 after being attacked and damaged by the destroyer *Yamagumo*.

Skate set up an attack on *Zuihō*, as the carriers left Truk. The formation changed course, however, and a hasty attack by *Skate* followed for which three hits were claimed. In reality, *Skate*'s torpedoes missed altogether. *Gunnel*, off Iwo Jima in the Volcano Islands, made contact on December 2. It, too, missed. Only *Sailfish* off Honshu remained between the carriers and Japan.

Sailfish was considered a hard-luck boat. One of ten Sargo-class boats, it was originally commissioned *Squalus*. On May 23, 1939, *Squalus* sank during a test dive: 26 of the crew drowned but 33 trapped survivors were rescued after *Sculpin* found *Squalus*. *Squalus* was re-floated, refitted, and recommissioned as *Sailfish*.

Sailfish was on its tenth war patrol. Over its first nine patrols it had sunk just three ships, a less-than-stellar performance. Many were convinced *Sailfish* was jinxed, dubbing it *"Squailfish."* It sailed on its tenth patrol with new officers, including a new captain, Lieutenant Commander Robert E.W. Ward. At first the "jinx" continued when a stern-tube torpedo had a hot run. The torpedo was manually

Sailfish was a Sargo-class boat that began its career as *Squalus*. After sinking during a diving test on May 23, 1939, it was re-floated in an operation shown here, just before it resurfaced. Repaired and refitted, it was recommissioned as *Sailfish*. (USNHHC)

ejected but the tube was unusable thereafter, restricting *Sailfish* to the use of seven torpedo tubes.

Ward moved *Sailfish* to intercept the three carriers as a typhoon moved through its patrol area. The boat surfaced at sunset on December 3 facing 50kn winds and towering seas. Near midnight, it made radar contact with the carrier force, 9,000yd distant. By 2355hrs, the boat's radar showed four pips: it had found the Ultra alert carrier force. The task force commander, working on the assumption that a typhoon made a submarine attack impossible, was not zigzagging to better deal with weather conditions.

The typhoon prevented *Sailfish* from making a standard surface approach. Ward dropped the boat to radar depth, with the SJ surface search radar antenna above water, and closed in. He picked the largest radar pip at 2,100yd. At 0012hrs, December 4, *Sailfish* launched four bow torpedoes. Ward was turning *Sailfish* to bring his stern-mounted torpedoes to bear when the four bow torpedoes reached *Chūyō*. Two hit.

As Ward set up the stern shots, the soundman reported approaching propellers. An escorting destroyer had spotted the four torpedo tracks and was rushing *Sailfish*. Ward ordered the boat deep, setting silent running, and was still descending at 0016hrs when the destroyer dropped depth charges. The first two landed close, but caused no real damage; 19 others landed increasingly farther away.

Sailfish stayed down until 0158hrs, during which time its bow torpedo tubes were reloaded. Rising to radar depth, the boat conducted a radar sweep, spotting multiple contacts. Ward assumed one of the contacts moving slowly was his previous target, damaged but not out. His assumption was correct: *Chūyō*, hit by two of *Sailfish*'s torpedoes forward, could still steam, but at reduced speed to prevent the forward bulkheads failing. The rest of the task force moved on. With a typhoon raging, its commander decided getting *Zuihō* and *Un'yō* safely home was more important than standing by *Chūyō*. A destroyer, *Urakaze*, was detailed to watch *Chūyō*. The two carriers, the cruiser *Maya*, and three destroyers, pushed on to Yokosuka.

Sailfish off Mare Island following an April 1943 refit. This shows the boat's appearance when it attacked and sank *Chūyō* on December 4, 1943. It was fitted with radar at the time, which it made use of for its first three attacks on the carrier. (USNHHC)

Chūyō, photographed while at anchor at Truk in April 1943, was one of several Japanese carriers regularly used to transport aircraft between the Home Islands and Truk. The aircraft were offloaded and flown to other Japanese airfields. (Sakai City Maritime History Science Museum/Wikimedia/Public Domain)

Sailfish tracked *Chūyō* and *Urakaze* by radar for over three hours. With dawn approaching, Ward decided to attack the unseen target once again. The rain had stopped, and the typhoon was dying away. At 0550hrs, with the range 3,200yd, he fired three more bow torpedoes. *Chūyō* was crawling at 1kn. Two of the torpedoes hit, this time opening up *Chūyō*'s boiler room and engine room. The badly damaged carrier lost power.

In response to the attack, *Chūyō* opened up with every one of its guns, firing wildly in the direction from which the torpedoes had come. *Urakaze* began dropping depth charges. Though it was apparent the Japanese did not know where *Sailfish* was, Ward took the boat deep one more time, which allowed the torpedo tubes to be reloaded.

Chūyō reported it was in danger of sinking. Preparations to abandon ship were made. The task force commander sent *Zuihō* and *Un'yō* to Japan with one destroyer escorting. He (in *Maya*) turned back to reach *Chūyō*, accompanied by the destroyer *Sazanami*, while the destroyer *Akebono* raced at full speed to *Chūyō*.

Once again *Sailfish* rose to periscope depth. The boat's SJ radar spotted the now-motionless *Chūyō*. Ward closed to 1,700yd, and at 0758hrs he finally glimpsed his previously unseen prey listing to port. At 0940hrs he fired three more torpedoes. Sonar reported tremendous explosions and "breaking up" noises, but waves prevented Ward from seeing the target through the periscope. Then Ward saw another ship, the onrushing *Maya*. Ward took *Sailfish* down to 90ft and used the boat's sonar to set up an attack on the cruiser; but by then it was retiring at high speed. Ward reported he felt he "threw away the chance of a lifetime."

At 1330hrs Ward took *Sailfish* up to periscope depth again and conducted a 360-degree search of the horizon. The ocean was empty. *Chūyō* had sunk hours earlier, the first Japanese aircraft carrier dispatched by a USN submarine. The destroyers and cruiser were gone. Ward was unsure *Chūyō* had sunk and not been towed away; but Vice Admiral Lockwood, then COMSUBPAC, *was* sure. Decoded Japanese radio traffic confirmed the kill. When *Sailfish* arrived home and tied up at the pier, Lockwood met Ward and awarded him the Navy Cross.

ALBACORE VS *TAIHŌ*, JUNE 19, 1944

After losses in the Solomon Islands, Japan's carriers largely withdrew from combat, training new carrier-qualified pilots and awaiting an opportunity to fight a single decisive battle to turn the tide of war back in Japan's favor. As the United States began preparations to take the Mariana Islands, Vice Admiral Ozawa Jisaburō, commanding the 1st Mobile Fleet, decided it was time to attack. Shortly after US airstrikes on the Marianas began on June 12, 1944, Japan's fleet sortied to meet US forces.

US codebreakers detected the sortie. COMSUBPAC had seven submarines deployed between the Philippines and the Marianas, waters the Japanese had to cross. The submarines were shifted to positions where intelligence indicated Japanese warships were most likely to pass. One of the boats was *Albacore*, a Gato-class boat on its ninth war patrol, commanded by Lieutenant Commander James W. Blanchard.

On June 18, COMSUBPAC shifted *Albacore* 100NM south from its patrol area to give a better chance of intercepting the Japanese fleet. At 0800hrs on June 19, Blanchard raised the periscope for a 360-degree sweep. The boat was in the middle of Ozawa's A Force: three carriers, two heavy cruisers, one light cruiser, and nine destroyers. The carriers of the 1st Carrier Division were approaching *Albacore*. The Japanese were launching an airstrike.

Blanchard let the lead carrier pass, selecting the second one (initially 9,000yd away) as his target. A destroyer moved across *Albacore*'s periscope crosshairs, between the boat and the second carrier. Blanchard let the destroyer pass and continued to track his target. *Albacore* closed range to 5,300yd. Then its TDC began misbehaving, giving obviously false information. Rather than abort the attack, Blanchard chose to revert to pre-TDC practice and depend on purely visual observations for the firing solution. To increase the odds of successfully hitting the target, just before 0900hrs all six of *Albacore*'s bow torpedoes were launched.

Albacore, attacked by three destroyers immediately after launching the torpedoes, dived before Blanchard could observe the attack's outcome. His "seaman's eye" was less accurate than a functioning TDC, but it was good enough to get a hit. Four torpedoes missed ahead. Two explosions were heard, one at the time torpedo No. 6 should have arrived at the carrier. *Albacore*'s bridge team thought they had one successful torpedo hit, maybe two. Thereafter they concentrated on surviving. Destroyers rained 25 depth charges on the boat, some close enough to flake cork insulation off the overhead.

Blanchard's target, which he identified as a Shōkaku-class aircraft carrier, was *Taihō*, Japan's newest and most powerful carrier. A development of the Shōkaku class, it was

Albacore heading back to the Pacific and war patrols following a refit at Mare Island Naval Shipyard in April 1944. Two months later, during the battle of the Philippine Sea, the boat would find and torpedo the carrier *Taihō*, which sank due to poor damage control. (USNHHC)

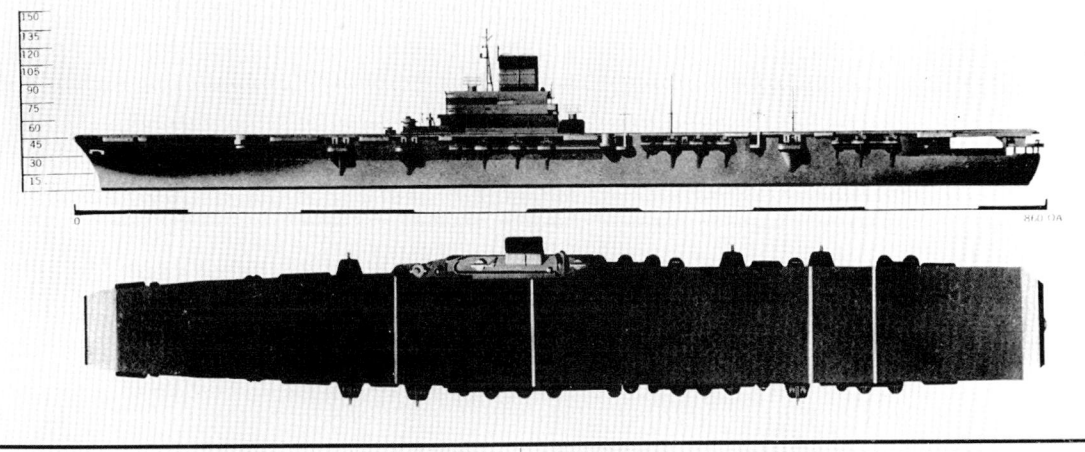

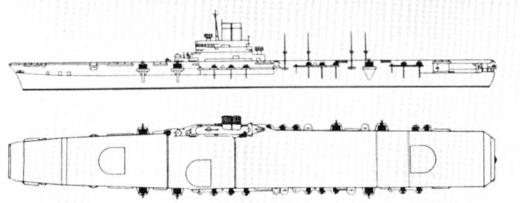

Length: 860' oa.

Beam: 100'—flight deck width.

Displacement: 35,000 tons (standard), estimated.

Armament: Max. Elev.   Range   Ceiling
12—5"/40 in twin mounts.   85°   15,260 yds. 33,000 ft.
Undetermined number of AAMG—probable triple mounts.

Plane capacity: 80 plus; 3 elevators.

Full speed: 33 knots (?).

heavily armored and compartmented; and its service with Ozawa's fleet was its first combat appearance.

One of *Albacore*'s torpedoes had hit *Taihō* abreast of the carrier's forward elevator. A second torpedo would have hit *Taihō* ahead of that one, but Warrant Officer Kumatsu Sakio, piloting an aircraft just launched from the carrier, spotted the torpedoes. He dove his aircraft onto one torpedo, exploding it 100yd short of its target, sacrificing himself for his carrier. Kumatsu's action should have worked – the warhead of a single US torpedo was not powerful enough to inflict serious damage on a carrier as well-protected as *Taihō* – but the remaining torpedo punched a hole in the carrier's side, which flooded the elevator well.

Taihō, down by the bow 5ft, continued steaming at 26kn. Concussion caused the elevator, at flight-deck level for launch operations, to drop 6ft and jam in position, thus suspending air-launch operations. Some of the forward aviation gasoline (avgas) tanks cracked. Saltwater and avgas flooded the elevator well. It was minor damage, however, and the flooding was quickly contained. Damage-control crews boarded over the elevator hole. By 0920hrs, air-launch operations resumed.

Previous Japanese carriers had open hangar decks; but *Taihō*'s builders had plated over the bow up to the flight deck. While protecting the hangar during rough seas, this feature had the additional effect of trapping gases. The leaking avgas, lighter than seawater, accumulated in the elevator well, floated to the surface, and began vaporizing. The boarded-over elevator trapped the avgas vapor in the hangar, creating a deadly fuel–air mix.

There were too few hatches to vent the fumes. Knocking out portholes, chopping holes in the bulwarks, and lowering the aft elevator to increase draft also failed to clear

The Office of Naval Intelligence Identification card for *Taihō*. The carrier was of new construction, just out of the dockyard at Kure, and there were few photographs of the vessel available. Lieutenant Commander Blanchard and his officers aboard *Albacore* used these cards for identification purposes. (USNHHC)

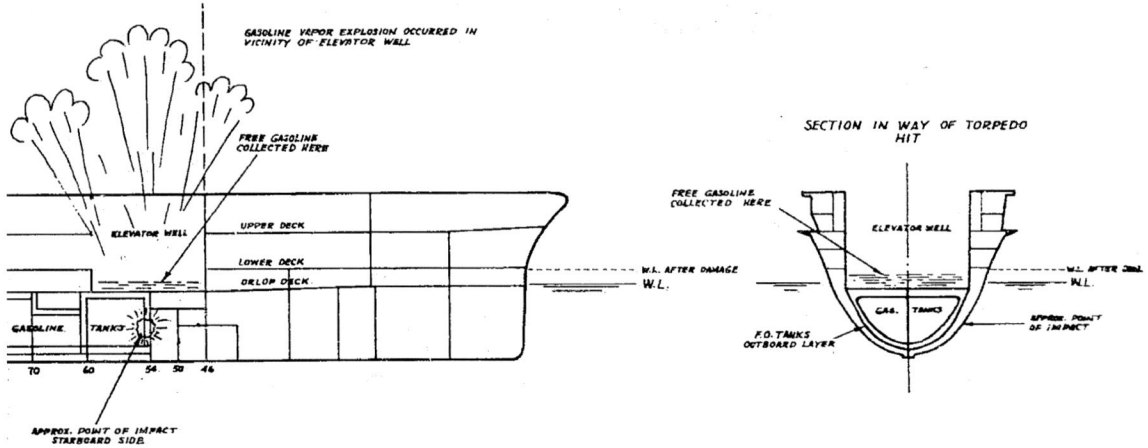

This diagram illustrates a postwar assessment of how *Taihō* sank. It shows how the torpedo hit permitted avgas to accumulate in the forward elevator well, and the catastrophic results of improperly ventilating the fumes. (AC)

them. The inexperienced damage-control officer finally ordered ventilation fans to be set on full power, with doors and hatches open to increase airflow. Avgas vapors filled the ship. Finally at 1430hrs, hours after being hit, a spark ignited the fuel–air mix. *Taihō* was wracked by a massive explosion. It blew out both sides of the carrier, which began to settle. Fire and flooding doomed *Taihō*, which sank two hours later.

Blanchard, however, was unaware of this; and when *Albacore* eventually surfaced, the seas were clear. The carriers, including *Taihō*, were already over 100NM east. Blanchard believed he had missed the opportunity of a lifetime. So did COMSUBPAC at Pearl Harbor. Blanchard was praised for carrying out an aggressive patrol and received a Commendation Ribbon for damaging a Shōkaku-class carrier. Naval Intelligence lost track of *Taihō* after the battle of the Philippine Sea, and it took months for them to realize the reason was that *Albacore*'s attack had in fact sunk *Taihō*. Blanchard's Commendation Ribbon was upgraded to a Navy Cross.

CAVALLA VS *SHŌKAKU*, JUNE 19, 1944

In June 1944 *Cavalla*, a new Gato-class boat, was on its first war patrol. Captained by Commander Herman J. Kossler on his sixth war patrol, but his first as captain, on June 15 the boat was headed to the San Bernardino Strait, to relieve *Flying Fish*. When *Flying Fish* spotted the Japanese fleet exiting the San Bernardino Strait and steaming east that day, *Cavalla*'s orders changed. COMSUBPAC sent the boat and *Piperfish* to positions 360NM east of the San Bernardino Strait to intercept the Japanese carrier force moving to oppose US landings on Saipan in the Marianas. Pre-invasion attacks against Japanese forces on the island had begun a few days previously.

Cavalla searched vainly for the Japanese carrier force throughout June 16. At 2303hrs, it picked up four ships: two oilers escorted by two destroyers, a support force to refuel warships. *Cavalla* attempted to attack, but was driven deep by one of the escorting destroyers. When *Cavalla* resurfaced the four ships were gone. *Cavalla* spent 13 hours the next day hunting the two oilers, but without success.

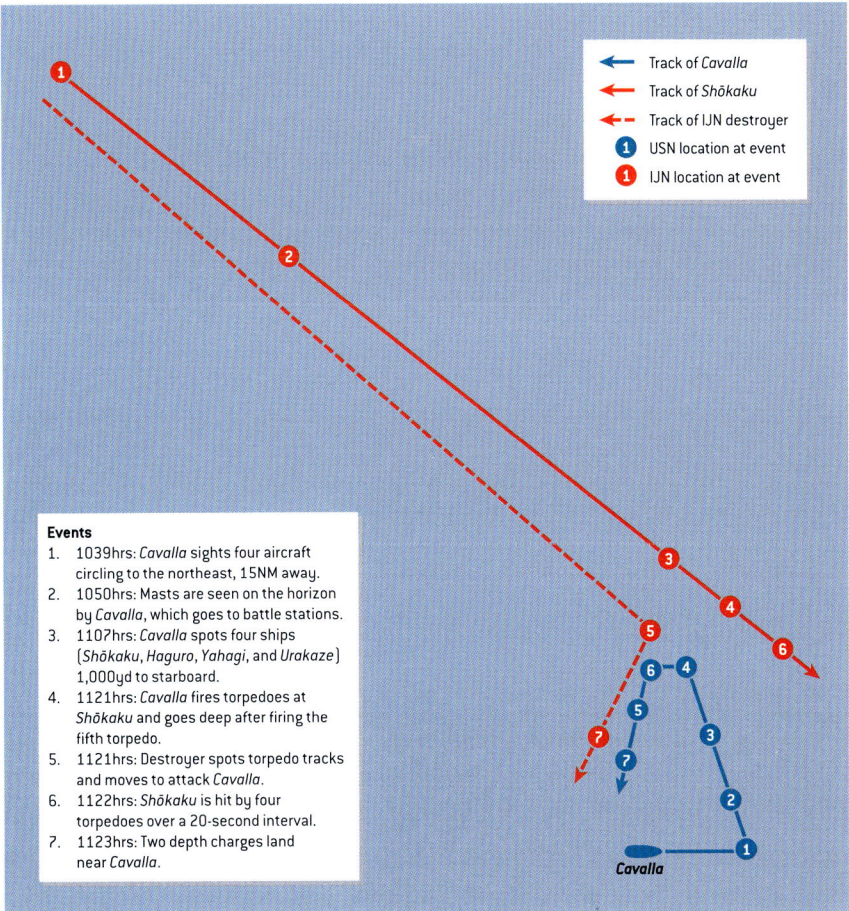

This map shows how *Cavalla* tracked down and sank *Shōkaku* during the battle of the Philippine Sea.

Legend:
- Track of *Cavalla*
- Track of *Shōkaku*
- Track of IJN destroyer
- USN location at event
- IJN location at event

Events
1. 1039hrs: *Cavalla* sights four aircraft circling to the northeast, 15NM away.
2. 1050hrs: Masts are seen on the horizon by *Cavalla*, which goes to battle stations.
3. 1107hrs: *Cavalla* spots four ships (*Shōkaku*, *Haguro*, *Yahagi*, and *Urakaze*) 1,000yd to starboard.
4. 1121hrs: *Cavalla* fires torpedoes at *Shōkaku* and goes deep after firing the fifth torpedo.
5. 1121hrs: Destroyer spots torpedo tracks and moves to attack *Cavalla*.
6. 1122hrs: *Shōkaku* is hit by four torpedoes over a 20-second interval.
7. 1123hrs: Two depth charges land near *Cavalla*.

Cavalla

At 2100hrs on June 17, *Cavalla*'s radar made contact with a fleet, seven large pips. Kossler assumed the Japanese fleet contained carriers, battleships, and cruisers. He was correct: it was Ozawa's A Force, 20,000yd distant. *Cavalla* submerged, moved to intercept, and determined the fleet contained several carriers. He opted to let the ships pass without attacking. Elmer "Zeke" Zelmer explained: "We had to watch it go by and report first, shoot second. If we waited until after we shot before we gave the report we might be sunk during that interval. Then no information would get out as to where our opposition was heading." Zelmer sent the contact report at 2245hrs.

Shōkaku in August 1941, shortly after it was commissioned. By 1944 its light antiaircraft armament had been increased significantly, and it had radar installed. Both features are missing in this photo. (USNHHC)

A photograph of *Cavalla* in 1945 entering Pearl Harbor at war's end. The boat sank *Shōkaku* on its first war patrol and spent the rest of the war in Australia. This photograph accurately shows the boat's configuration at the battle of the Philippine Sea. (AC)

COMSUBPAC responded, signaling, "Hang on and trail as long as possible regardless of fuel expenditure." The opportunity to attack was gone. Zelmer said:

> When we missed the two tankers we tried to attack morale went down, down, down. When the fleet came over the horizon and we had to submerge and let it go by and report it helped morale and we wanted to do something. Reporting it was fine but it really wasn't what we really wanted to do. So our morale was very low before the actual fight when we sank the *Shōkaku*.

On the morning of June 19, *Cavalla* and its crew got another chance. That morning the boat was "on the surface initially," Zelmer related. "Then we were forced down by an airplane. We stayed down for a while, and then came back to the surface. As we came up we could see four small planes circling in the distance. Sonar was able to hear noises in that direction. We headed in that direction and the targets came at us very, very quickly." Kossler later wrote: "The picture was too good to be true." Ozawa's

Cavalla, stopped at Saipan, having refueled from a tanker after sinking *Shōkaku*. While there, Lieutenant Commander Kossler (center) gave a press conference about the action. (USNHHC)

A Force was heading toward them, conducting flight operations. Zelmer picked up the story:

They were making about 25 knots. We submerged when they got close enough we might get detected. Of course we were concerned about airplanes.

We began to track them by radar. We submerged to radar depth, so we had radar contact. That gave us the observations initially. Then skipper took over the periscope. We got close enough we felt we had to submerge to periscope depth. They were coming closer and they had to vary their course somewhat. It didn't come straight on. We were concerned that they might zig away from us, but during the latter phase of the attack when we submerged, they started going straight ahead to take airplanes on board they had sent out earlier. That helped us.

The skipper's periscope observations were very, very good. I plotted the first position and the second position several minutes later. I came up with a speed of 25 knots and a course direction. We zeroed in on that position and the course we ended up firing on, based on the first two observations by periscope.

Kossler fired six torpedoes and went deep. Zelmer continued:

There were three destroyers to worry about. One in particular on our side, so we went in quiet, went to silent running. All hands were at their battle positions. We got in to about 1,200 yards when the observations completed. As we were taking the next-to-last observations we saw the Japanese flag as we got close. We took the next observation. Then we fired six torpedoes.

We had some problems with that. The first five torpedoes went out with a spread shot. One torpedo should have passed ahead of the carrier, one behind it, and four through the middle. We fired six torpedoes but as we were firing the fifth torpedo, the destroyer turned directly towards us, Skipper took sight of him and decided it was now time to go deep. We continued firing the fifth one.

The next torpedo hung up in the tube and wouldn't come out. We were having it running hot in the tube. We were trying to claw for depth with the destroyer coming our way. Finally we launched the torpedo in place, where the firing command was given in the tube. The torpedo swam out and swam away. It probably was erratic.

We got down to about 150 feet as the destroyer came directly over us from astern and dropped four depth charges. And then the depth charging began for the next 2½ hours. We took 106 depth charges flung around us.

We flooded the main induction trunk [the intake for the diesels when on the surface]. That induction trunk is about 36 inches in diameter and runs aft to the engine room. It's about 100 feet long. The water in there weighed 15 tons. We were heavy by that amount.

We also had water in the forward torpedo room. One of the poppet tank valves that was supposed to shut the tank overflowed into the bilge in the forward torpedo room.

Kossler's firing solution was dead on. Four torpedoes struck *Shōkaku* when it was most vulnerable – during flight operations. *Shōkaku* had survived serious damage in two previous battles, but this time the damage caused by the four torpedo hits was fatal. Massive explosions wracked the carrier. Uncontrollable fires followed. At 1100hrs it fell out of formation. At 1510hrs it capsized and sank.

OVERLEAF

Shōkaku was struck by four of the six torpedoes launched by *Cavalla*. The first torpedo to hit struck forward of the carrier's island where aviation gasoline (avgas) was stored. The shock of the torpedo explosion cracked the avgas storage tanks, allowing the volatile fuel to escape. It almost immediately ignited, resulting in a massive fire. The second torpedo struck seconds later, at the bulkhead separating Firerooms 3 and 5. This fractured plates on both sides of the bulkhead, causing both firerooms to flood. The third torpedo hit was under the island and flooded the bomb magazine and torpedo storage area. The fourth and final torpedo hit was at the bow. There was nothing critically important at this location, but it cost the carrier buoyancy forward, leading it to sink by the bow when it finally went down. The combined effect of the four torpedo hits on *Shōkaku* was devastating. Two of the carrier's eight firerooms were flooded and the boilers in several others knocked off-line, curtailing power available for firefighting. The leaking avgas ignited into fires that quickly became uncontrollable, and the hit near the magazine forced the magazines to be flooded. *Shōkaku* sank four hours after being hit. This plate depicts *Shōkaku* at the instant the second torpedo hit. Avgas fires resulting from the first torpedo hit have already started, and a towering plume of water is rising where the second torpedo is striking. Three other torpedoes can be seen streaking toward *Shōkaku*, two of which will hit.

ARCHERFISH VS *SHINANO*, NOVEMBER 29, 1944

On December 28, 1944, *Archerfish* was patrolling the approaches to Tokyo Bay. It was the boat's fifth combat patrol. The most significant result of its previous four patrols was the rescue of one naval aviator during lifeguard duty off Iwo Jima in July 1944. The boat had not sunk or damaged any Japanese ships previously.

After four fruitless patrols Vice Admiral Lockwood, COMSUBPAC, replaced *Archerfish's* skipper with Lieutenant Commander Joseph F. Enright in September 1944. Enright, who had asked to be relieved as captain after an unproductive first patrol commanding *Dace*, was given a rare second command opportunity. He was determined to make the most of it.

At 0848hrs on November 29, *Archerfish's* radar picked up a contact at 24,700yd exiting Tokyo Bay, heading south at 20kn. Enright assumed it was a lightly loaded large tanker; but when he closed he realized his contact was a carrier, the biggest he had ever seen. It was *Shinano*. Originally intended as the third Yamato-class battleship, after the battle of Midway, the IJN General Staff converted the vessel being built in Yokosuka Naval Arsenal to a carrier. The battleship hull, complete when the decision was made, was kept as built, with an armor belt up to 400mm (15.75in) thick. On October 8, 1944, two years after the decision, the new carrier was launched, unfinished. When it sailed, four of the 12 boilers didn't work, pumps and watertight doors required installation, and much other work remained before it could be commissioned.

On November 24, the United States Army Air Forces (USAAF) began conducting Boeing B-29 Superfortress long-range bombing raids on Tokyo from bases in the Marianas. Raids on November 27 and 29 hit Tokyo's docks. The IJN General Staff was concerned Yokosuka might be next, and wanted *Shinano* moved to a safer location. The IJN General Staff decided to complete *Shinano* at Kure Naval Yard, in the Inland Sea. Another perceived advantage of Kure Naval Arsenal was its workers were considered more skilled than those at Yokosuka Naval Arsenal.

Shinano's commander, Captain Abe Toshio, asked for a few days' delay to train the carrier's green crew. His request was denied. *Shinano* was carrying six *Shin'yō* suicide boats and 50 Yokusaka MXY-7 *Ohka* rocket-powered manned flying bombs to be rush-delivered to the Philippines; but when Abe discovered he could not get air cover, he decided to sail that evening, shortly after sundown, escorted by four destroyers. It was a 16-hour trip to Kure.

Archerfish departing San Francisco Bay in 1945, following a refit after it sank *Shinano*. (AC)

Because of *Shinano's* speed, *Archerfish* could not keep up while submerged. Enright surfaced *Archerfish* and began pursuing. The boat's top speed when surfaced was 20kn, the speed *Shinano* was making. Enright steered a straight line parallel to the carrier's direction of travel. The carrier and destroyers were zigzagging. At 2322hrs, *Shinano* slowed to 18kn due to an overheating shaft bearing. *Archerfish* slowly pulled even with then ahead of the carrier, which he thought might escape. As a precaution, Enright sent COMSUBPAC two contact reports, hoping another submarine could intercept.

At 0300hrs, six hours into the chase, *Shinano* turned on to an intercept course with *Archerfish*. At 0308hrs, Enright took the boat down in preparation for the attack. At 0316hrs, *Archerfish* began firing four bow torpedoes and two stern torpedoes at *Shinano*, then 1,500yd away. The first hit 47 seconds later. Five more hits followed, two of which were observed by Enright.

An IJN destroyer, 500yd away, saw *Archerfish* and made an attack run. Enright took the boat deep, to 400ft, and stayed down until 0610hrs, when he came up to periscope depth. A 360-degree sweep of the horizon revealed an empty sea. Enright believed he had sunk *Shinano* at that spot.

In reality *Shinano* continued steaming at 18kn after absorbing six torpedo hits. Abe was not seriously worried: the carrier's half-sister, the battleship *Musashi*, had taken 19 torpedoes before sinking at the battle of Leyte Gulf on October 24. Abe thought *Shinano* could safely make Kure.

If complete, *Shinano* likely would have successfully completed the trip, but many access hatches were open to allow construction workers passage. Some watertight doors awaited installation and none had been leak-checked. As a result, damage-control parties could not contain the flooding that resulted from damage caused by the six torpedo hits. Inexperienced, they did not realize the perilous state *Shinano* was in until it was too late. The carrier began listing, threatening to capsize. Counterflooding was ordered to correct the list.

As *Shinano* took on water, it settled deeper, increasing water pressure and water inrush. At 0900hrs, the engine rooms flooded. By 1018hrs, with a list of 30 degrees, Abe ordered *Shinano* abandoned. At 1057hrs, the doomed carrier capsized and sank, taking over 1,400 men down with it; a further 1,040 were rescued. Abe chose to go down with the carrier.

When Enright returned to Guam on December 15, US Naval Intelligence was skeptical of his claim to have sunk a carrier. *Shinano*, having been built in secret, was not on any US list of Japanese carriers. Despite these misgivings Enright was eventually credited with sinking a 20,000-ton carrier. The full story came out only after war's end. Then the tonnage was upped to 59,000 tons, giving *Archerfish* the best patrol by tonnage of any USN submarine.

Shinano, photographed during its first and final sea voyage. The tanker silhouette painted on its side can be seen, albeit poorly due to the low resolution of the photograph. (Kure City Maritime History and Science Museum/ Wikimedia/Public Domain)

STATISTICS AND ANALYSIS

There were at least 67 encounters between USN submarines and Japanese carriers in World War II. There may have been more, but these would have been incidental encounters in which a submarine spotted a carrier in the distance but was not able to engage, or the carrier was misidentified as a tanker and reported as such. (Viewed through a periscope, carriers, tankers, and large tenders were easily confused.)

In 22 contacts the submarine was unable to launch torpedoes at the carrier. In six of these contacts the submarine was forced to submerge by Japanese aircraft or escort warships before getting close enough to attack. In one case (*Cavalla*'s encounter with A Force on June 18, 1944), the submarine's captain avoided attacking in order to make a contact report. He correctly felt reporting the position of the enemy immediately prior to an expected surface action was more important than attacking. In 15 other cases the submarine spotted, but could not close with the carrier group. These groups typically cruised at 18–20kn, preventing a surfaced chase.

Of the remaining encounters, ten sank a carrier, 12 damaged a carrier seriously enough for it to require dockyard repairs (in one case rendering the carrier a constructive total loss), and 22 failed to damage the carrier. In seven of the latter cases the torpedoes either prematurely exploded before reaching the target, or hit the target carrier but failed to explode. (Dud torpedo hits occurred in three attacks in which other torpedoes hit and damaged the target carrier.) In wargaming parlance, if a USN fleet submarine encountered a Japanese carrier it had roughly a one-sixth chance of sinking it, a one-sixth chance of damaging it, a two-sixth chance of missing it altogether, and a two-sixth chance of failing to be able to carry out an attack.

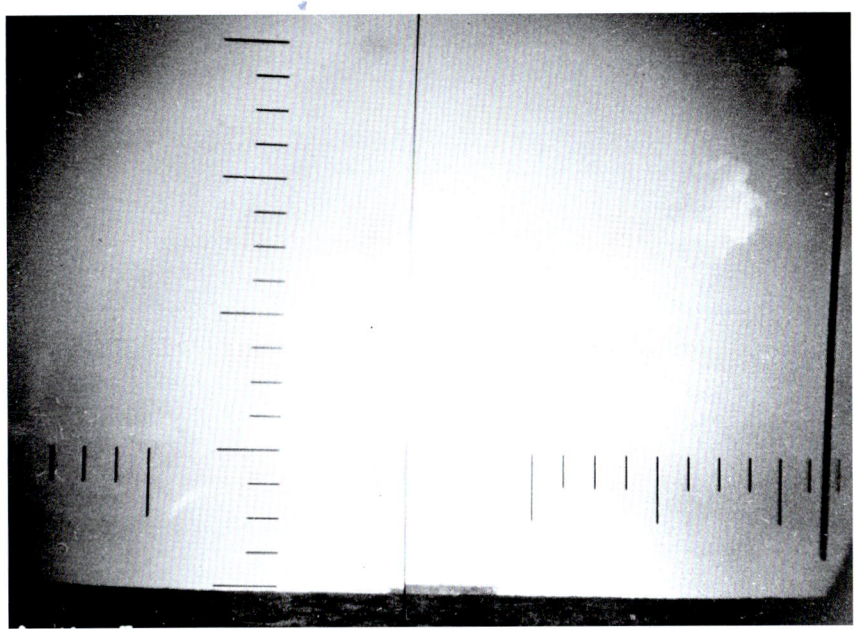

This periscope view of a Taiyō-class aircraft carrier illustrates the difficulty of target identification through a periscope, even when the seas are relatively calm. (USNHHC)

The last US dud or prematurely exploding torpedo launched against a Japanese carrier was recorded in October 1943, two months prior to *Sailfish* sinking *Chūyō*. It took that long to wring out all the torpedo issues. Bad torpedoes were an issue prior to then, however. *Nautilus*, in its attack against the stationary *Kaga*, had two torpedoes miss (probably due to magnetic exploder issues or torpedoes running deep), one prematurely exploded, and one was a dud hit. It was a hat trick of torpedo failures.

Not until September 28, 1942, after nine months of war, did a USN fleet submarine damage a Japanese carrier, when *Trout* caught *Taiyō* off Truk. *Trout's* captain, the aggressive Lieutenant Commander Lawson P. "Red" Ramage, scored only one hit with the five torpedoes fired at close range. The other four probably ran deep or had magnetic exploder problems.

USN submarine effectiveness increased dramatically after the torpedo problems were fixed. Prior to *Sailfish* sinking *Chūyō* on December 4, 1943, seven Japanese carriers were damaged in 40 encounters. From December 1943 through December 1944, 15 carriers were hit in 30 encounters – a 50 percent success rate – with ten carriers sunk.

These encounters were usually not random: 28 encounters, roughly 40 percent, occurred due to COMSUBPAC radio orders positioning USN fleet submarines in the path of Japanese carriers as a result of fleet sighting by other submarines (such as *Flying Fish* reporting the passage of Ozawa's A Force through the San Bernardino Strait) or Ultra alerts. Decryption of Japanese message traffic by USN codebreakers resulted in Ultra alerts. While COMSUBPAC never kept USN submarines as tightly controlled as Großadmiral Karl Dönitz did Kriegsmarine (German Navy) U-boats, he never hesitated to send them intelligence to help them sink carriers. Three sinkings resulted from these Ultra alerts.

No USN submarine managed to sink more than one Japanese carrier; and all ten carriers sunk were the victims of attacks by different boats. Only 11 boats had multiple encounters with carriers: *Albacore, Cavalla, Crevalle, Dace, Haddock, Hake, Redfish, Sculpin,* and *Steelhead* had two each: *Halibut* and *Trigger* had three each. *Redfish* was the only boat to hit two Japanese carriers and the last to sink one. It turned *Jun'yō* into a total constructive loss on December 9, 1944, and sank *Unryū* ten days later, during its second war patrol. *Albacore, Cavalla,* and *Hake* each sank one carrier in one of their encounters, but came up empty on the other. (*Hake* sank the IJA aircraft carrier/transport *Nigitsu Maru* on January 12, 1944, but missed a Shōkaku-class carrier three months later.) *Haddock* damaged *Un'yō* on January 19, 1944. *Crevalle, Dace, Sculpin,* and *Steelhead* failed to score in each of their two encounters.

Halibut encountered *Un'yō* twice, in July 1943 and January 1944. It shot at the carrier in the first encounter, but hit auxiliary cruiser *Aikoku Maru* instead. It also torpedoed *Jun'yō* in November 1943. *Trigger*'s three encounters all occurred on its fifth war patrol in April–June 1943 off Tokyo Bay. It was unable to get into an attack position on Admiral Mineichi Koga's carriers the first two occasions it encountered them, but the third attempt proved lucky and damaged escort carrier *Hiyō* on June 10. *Trigger* could have sunk *Hiyō*, but of the four torpedoes fired two prematurely exploded, one was a dud, and only one hit and exploded. Four hits would have put *Hiyō* under.

The crew of *Trigger* pose with a flag they created to celebrate their successful attack on *Hiyō* made on June 10, 1943. The flag shows four hits. Although four explosions were heard, only two torpedoes exploded before reaching *Hiyō* and a third hit, but was a dud. (USNHHC)

Un'yō was a frequent target of USN fleet submarines, being successfully attacked twice. It is shown here in early February 1944 after being torpedoed by *Haddock* on January 19 and damaged by a storm, after which it returned to Kure Naval Arsenal for repairs. (Akira Furikawa/ Wikimedia/Public Domain)

Seven Japanese carriers (*Akitsu Maru*, *Chūyō*, *Nigitsu Maru*, *Shinano*, *Shin'yō*, *Taihō*, and *Unryū*) had only one known encounter with a USN submarine, but all were sunk as a result. Two carriers that were significantly luckier in their meetings with USN submarines were *Zuikaku* and *Zuihō*, both of which were undamaged in two encounters, but later sunk by aircraft. *Zuihō* was hit in one of two submarine attacks on it, but the torpedo was a dud.

Hiyō was less lucky. It encountered USN submarines three times, but was missed twice and only damaged when fired at by *Trigger*. *Taiyō* also had three clashes with submarines. The first time, in May 1942, the torpedoes prematurely exploded before reaching *Taiyō*. The second time, *Trout* damaged the carrier. Finally, *Rasher* sank it on August 18, 1944.

USN submarines encountered *Un'yō* four times. The first time, *Un'yō* escaped damage because the torpedoes intended for it hit *Aikoku Maru* instead. The second time, on January 19, 1944, *Haddock* badly damaged *Un'yō* when the carrier steamed into torpedoes that had been fired at *Shōkaku*. A few days later, *Halibut* attempted to sink the damaged *Un'yō*, but could not get into an attack position. After repairs *Un'yō* was off Hong Kong on September 16, 1944, when *Barb* found and sank the carrier.

Shōkaku had no fewer than seven encounters with USN submarines. It escaped damage in six of the clashes, three in 1942 and three in 1944, including when *Un'yō* steamed into torpedoes fired at *Shōkaku*. In all the other four clashes the submarines could not establish a good attack position. Finally it was sunk by *Cavalla* on June 19, 1944.

Jun'yō also had seven encounters. The carrier avoided damage on four occasions, once on November 3, 1944, when the destroyer *Akikaze* interposed, deliberately taking the torpedoes *Pintado* had fired at the carrier, and sinking as a result. *Jun'yō* was damaged on three occasions: the first on November 5, 1943 by *Halibut*; the second on December 8, 1944, when *Sea Devil* torpedoed it; and again the next day, when *Redfish* critically damaged it.

These numbers are uncertain, however, because USN submarines reported 15 encounters with unidentified aircraft carriers and four with "Shōkaku-class" carriers (which may or may not have been Shōkaku class).

All successful attacks followed a pattern. They almost always started with the submarine surfaced, with the enemy detected by either visual or radar observation. (Lieutenant Commander Blanchard surfaced to periscope depth to find *Albacore* in the midst of the Japanese fleet, but his doing so was an exception.) As it closed, the submarine submerged, to make the final run-in under water, to help avoid detection. The submarine had to evade escorts on the way in.

Typically, the attack was made at close range (2,400–1,200yd) and a full spread of torpedoes was fired. This minimized enemy reaction time, because torpedoes could be evaded with sufficient warning. Finally, immediately after the attack the submarine went deep, without waiting to observe the hit. A depth-charging typically followed; often it went on for hours. The result was the submarine's captain and crew were often unable to assess the actual damage or what they had actually hit. *Cavalla*'s crew assumed they sank the carrier they torpedoed because, as Zelmer reported, "About 2½ hours later we heard some distant explosions and a rumbling that carried on for some seconds."

At about the same time Blanchard heard "a distant and persistent explosion of great force," followed by a second. He was sure it was *Taihō*, which *Albacore* had torpedoed. Both boats were convinced it was their kill. (Based on time, it was probably *Shōkaku*.) Similarly, Lieutenant Commander Enright was convinced *Shinano* sank where he torpedoed it. In reality, the carrier steamed off at its top available speed only to sink later. The truth of these and other claims were not sorted out until after war's end.

Poor Japanese damage control contributed to USN success. Neither *Taihō* nor *Shinano* would have sunk had the ships' damage-control teams been more effective; and *Chūyō* might have escaped had its damage-control team been quicker shoring up bulkheads after the first torpedo hit. If it could have steamed faster it might have cleared the area before *Sailfish* resurfaced.

Persistence usually paid off. *Sailfish*'s tenacity allowed it to sink *Chūyō*. Had Lieutenant Commander Ward called it a night after the first attack, *Chūyō* would have made it to Yokosuka. Had he quit after the second attack, the carrier might have been successfully towed to port. Similarly, Enright's tenacious pursuit of *Shinano* finally gave him an opportunity to make an attack.

CONCLUSION

Only five Japanese carriers survived to war's end. Only *Hōshō* and *Katsuragi* were capable of seagoing operations and faced USN submarines. *Jun'yō* and *Ryūhō* were floating wrecks, while *Ibuki* was still incomplete. All five carriers were scrapped between 1946 and 1949.

The United States lost 52 submarines in World War II. Surprisingly, none were lost attacking Japanese carriers. In large part this was because the escorts of the fast-moving Japanese carrier task forces could not stay with a submarine long enough to ensure its destruction. If the submarine evaded the first attack, it could outwait its attackers.

Of the 50-odd USN submarines that encountered Japanese carriers in the Pacific, ten were sunk in combat after their final, fatal meeting. This included *Albacore*, which sank *Taihō*; *Trout*, which damaged *Taiyō*; and *Trigger*, which torpedoed *Hiyō*.

Of the nine USN submarines that sank a Japanese carrier and survived the war, only *Cavalla* exists today, preserved at Seawolf Park in Galveston, Texas. It is open to visitors. *Drum*, which damaged *Ryūhō* on December 12, 1942, is similarly preserved at Battleship Memorial Park in Mobile, Alabama. The rest have all been scrapped.

The submarines of the prewar classes, which included *Sailfish*, were all scrapped in the immediate postwar years prior to 1950. The Gato class was effectively obsolete in 1946, and should have been scrapped, but the hulls were too new. Many were retained and converted into hunter-killer submarines and training submarines. In addition to *Cavalla*, *Rasher* became a research submarine before becoming a training boat. *Hake* remained unmodified in the reserve fleet as a training vessel. *Barb* underwent GUPPY conversion in the 1950s and was loaned to Italy before being returned in the 1970s. All but *Cavalla* were scrapped in the late 1970s.

Surprisingly, they outlasted the newer Balao-class boats, largely because the latter had been selected for training purposes. *Queenfish*, *Spadefish*, *Archerfish*, and *Redfish*

A photo of the reserve fleet at Mare Island, California, in January 1946. Among the 52 Gato- and Balao- class submarines in this photo is *Spadefish* (third row from the top, fifth from the right), which sank *Shin'yō* on November 17, 1944. (AC)

remained in USN service through the 1950s before being reclassified as auxiliary submarines in the early 1960s. By then they were obsolete, having been supplanted by nuclear-powered attack submarines. *Redfish* became a movie star in 1954, appearing in Disney's *20,000 Leagues Under the Sea*. In the 1958 movie *Run Silent, Run Deep* it featured as the fictional USS *Nerka* in exterior scenes. All the surviving Balao-class boats were scrapped or expended as targets in the 1960s.

Ultimately, USN fleet submarines dealt Japanese carriers a great deal more punishment than they received in reply. Attacking capital ships was the job for which these submarines were designed. Although that proved a secondary role for the fleet submarine in World War II, it was one at which they excelled. They were so good at this job that by the end of 1944 they turned the seagoing Japanese carrier into an endangered species. Speed proved inadequate protection for the carriers. Limited Japanese ASW capabilities and inadequate damage control left the carriers vulnerable to USN submarines.

BIBLIOGRAPHY

For the battles described in this book I relied heavily on Clay Blair Jr.'s excellent *Silent Victory* and various volumes of Samuel Eliot Morison's *History of United States Naval Operations in World War II*, which focused on the Pacific Theater. Morison is less than usually reliable when it comes to describing individual actions (for example, he claims *Nautilus* sank *Sōryū*), but is valuable for including the submariner's point of view. His errors were eliminated when cross-referenced with other sources (such as Blair).

In 2014 I was able to interview Elmer "Zeke" Zelmer, communications officer aboard *Cavalla* when it sank *Shōkaku*. That previously unpublished interview contributed to this book.

Numerous USN publications also contributed to this book. For Japanese technical details I used the "1945-46 US Naval Technical Mission to Japan" reports. Websites consulted include:

http://www.combinedfleet.com/
http://www.navweaps.com/
https://navsource.org/

The main books used were:

Blair, Clay Jr. (1975). *Silent Victory: The US Submarine War Against Japan*. New York, NY: J. Lippincott Co.

Chesneau, Roger (1984). *Aircraft Carriers of the World, 1914 to the Present: An Illustrated Encyclopedia*. London: Arms and Armour Press.

Enright, Joseph F. with Ryan, James W. (1988). *Shinano! The Sinking of Japan's Secret Supership*. New York, NY: St. Martin's Press.

Friedman, Norman (1981). *Naval Radar*. Annapolis, MD: Naval Institute Press.

Friedman, Norman (1995). *U.S. Submarines Through 1945: An Illustrated Design History*. Annapolis, MD: Naval Institute Press.

King, Ernest J. (1946). *U.S. Navy at War 1941–1945: Official Reports to the Secretary of the Navy*. Washington, DC: United States Navy Department.

Lengerer, Hans & Lars Ahlberg (2023). *Shokaku-Class Aircraft Carriers In the Imperial Japanese Navy during World War II*. Atglen, PA: Schiffer Publishing.

Moore, Stephen L. (2023). *Strike of the Sailfish: Two Sister Submarines and the Sinking of a Japanese Aircraft Carrier*. New York, NY: Dutton-Caliber.

Morison, Samuel Eliot (1949). *History of United States Naval Operations in World War II, Volume 4: Coral Sea, Midway, and Submarine Actions: May 1942–August 1942*. Boston, MA: Little, Brown.

Morison, Samuel Eliot (1951). *History of United States Naval Operations in World War II, Volume 7: Aleutians, Gilberts, and Marshalls: June 1942–April 1944*. Boston, MA: Little, Brown.

Morison, Samuel Eliot (1953). *History of United States Naval Operations in World War II, Volume 8: New Guinea and the Marianas: March 1944–August 1944*. Boston, MA: Little, Brown.

Morison, Samuel Eliot (1958). *History of United States Naval Operations in World War II, Volume 12: Leyte: June 1944–January 1945*. Boston, MA: Little, Brown.

Nakagawa Yasuzo (1997). *Japanese Radar and Related Weapons*. Laguna Hills, CA: Aegean Park Press.

United States Navy (1940). *The Bluejackets' Manual, 1940, Tenth Edition*. Annapolis, MD: US Naval Institute.

Cavalla, the only surviving submarine to have sunk a Japanese carrier, is a museum exhibit today, on display at Seawolf Park in Galveston, Texas. It no longer has its World War II appearance, having been altered to an attack submarine in the 1950s. (AC)

INDEX

References to illustrations are shown in **bold**.